AN OPINIONATED GUIDE

Folk Art

HOXTON MINI PRESS

What is

folk art?

In the simplest terms, it is art made by common folk rather than elite artists. It's a dizzyingly broad definition, encompassing a variety of art neglected by mainstream institutions. But there are shared features: historically made by people outside art schools, folk art often makes creative use of everyday media. It may have flattened perspectives, bold forms and vibrant colours. It is often domestic, created with a use in mind, such as clothing, toys or woodcraft, and rooted in community, engaging with traditions passed down through generations.

Everyday people have been creating art since the beginning of time, but 'folk art' wasn't coined until the 19th century. As Western society industrialised, nostalgia for handmade crafts grew. Folk art was seen as rustic, goodhearted and quirky, made by self-taught artists in rural societies. Yet its rise also coincided with colonial pursuits and art movements that essentialised non-Western works as raw and authentic. In this sense, folk art can be a controversial, externally imposed term that idealises the past and oversimplifies other cultures.

Where folk art begins and ends is blurry. It overlaps with 'outsider art' and 'naive art', practised by self-taught artists emulating a childlike style. The 20th and 21st centuries have eroded distinctions between elite and popular art, and folk art has found its way into galleries, auction houses and private collections. Contemporary folk artists are often labelled as such for their focus on folk culture and heritage, rather than because of exclusion from institutions.

And because it spans countless regional specificities, one could really speak about folk *arts*: there's no single manifesto or founding members here, but a constellation of art production. Folk art is as visceral and dazzling as our timeless desire to honour who we are and where we come from.

Why care

about

folk art?

It's tempting to consider art as something distinct from everyday life, created by so-called geniuses who have transcended the rest of us to make something astonishingly beautiful or enlightening. Historically, artistic masterpieces are kept in intimidating galleries, watched over by security staff.

Folk art empowers us to look beyond prestigious institutions and see art in everyday objects and scenes. Ordinary people have created remarkable work for generations, often anonymously. From samplers to quilts, board games to baskets, hand-carved dolls to sketches on scraps of cardboard, folk art encompasses objects kept at home or gifted to family and friends, bartered, worn or used daily – not often intended to be exhibited under Plexiglas and museum lights. It gives us valuable insight into the thoughts, desires, fears and lives of our ancestors and neighbours. Some of these insights are timeless: we have always used art to convey powerful tales and legends, process trauma, honour religious belief and express love. Others reveal surprisingly radical, ambitious and cross-cultural sentiments for time periods too easily dismissed as simple or isolated. Some folk artworks feel strikingly relatable; others challenge us to engage with unfamiliar cultures and practices. Deeply local and global at the same time, folk art invites curiosity and understanding. Artworks carry the warmth of a crackling bonfire, a place to gather and share stories.

By engaging with ancient traditions, contemporary folk artists invite us to challenge preconceived ideas about what constitutes art and what ought to be preserved and depicted. The canon – mostly dead, mostly white, mostly male – may be a dusty catalogue, largely unchanged over centuries, but folk art is a living, dynamic record of our shared humanity.

The short

story of

folk art

Cave paintings and petroglyphs *Prehistoric era*

Looking for ancient art often means unearthing work that may seem rudimentary to our modern eyes. But think again. Cave paintings and petroglyphs (carvings) often show mesmerising doodles of animals and pastoral or shamanic scenes. These sensitive records of human life predate 'folk art' as a concept, but they belong to the long history of art created by ordinary people about their everyday lives.

Ancient civilisations *20,000 BCE–500 CE*

The ancient Greek, Roman, Egyptian, Mesopotamian, Nasca, Inca, Chinese and many more civilisations left us with ceramic vessels (such as a surprising dog-shaped bottle, p.26), handheld mirrors, votive statuettes (p.20), elegant combs and other delicate and expressive objects. Crafted using various techniques – metalworking, woodturning, weaving and pottery – and often decorated with dyes and gems, they demonstrate a mastery of form and commitment to beauty as well as utility. Only the most durable of those are known to us today.

Medieval religious folk art *500s–1500s*

In the West, trinkets, amulets, icons and practical objects such as ivory boxes (p.36) were adorned with Christian devotional imagery and scenes that recalled popular tales, such as those of the Arthurian legends. In the Islamic world, spirituality was expressed through geometric and symmetrical patterns, which also added texture and dimension to glazed ceramics, brass and copper utensils, elevating these functional objects into ornaments (see incense burner, p.30). As people moved and traded, styles cross-fertilised.

Commonfolk portraits *1500s–1600s*

Painters in the West were traditionally academically trained and served wealthy patrons. This began to change when artists such as the anonymous Master of the Canesso Peddler (p.40) eschewed the traditional biblical scenes, regal and aristocratic portraits to focus instead on everyday folk. A distinct folk 'genre' developed through the work of Dutch Masters Pieter Bruegel the Elder (p.38) and Jan Steen (*Village Revel*, 1679), who turned their focus to peasant scenes and folk culture.

The rise of the decorative arts *1600s–1700s*

Renaissance art of Europe made a distinction between fine arts (visual art judged only on its aesthetic and intellectual content) and the decorative arts – beautified practical and functional objects, such as ornate, pocket-sized sewing scissors (p.42). In the emerging urban culture of Edo-period Japan (1603–1868), folk craftsmanship like woodblock prints (p.46) and kites (p.92) became hugely popular.

Folk Art Americana *1700s–1850s*

Itinerant artists like Ammi Phillips (p.54) and Erastus Salisbury Field travelled across the Northeastern United States painting portraits for the provincial middle class. These works became synonymous with American Folk Art, along with quilts (p.64), weathervanes and whirligigs (p.78), samplers (p.52), ornamental furniture and trade signs. They often embodied a wholesome, rural feel, as the newly independent Republic sought to define its cultural identity and celebrate communities such as the Amish, Shaker and the Pennsylvania Dutch (while relegating Native American cultural production).

The Arts and Crafts Movement *1860s–1910*

In Britain, the Arts and Crafts Movement emerged as a reaction to industrialisation. Intellectuals such as Thomas Carlyle, William Morris and John Ruskin linked the soul of a nation with its craftsmanship, arguing against the industrial processes that separated the design of an object from its physical manufacture. Proponents of the movement founded the Arts and Crafts Exhibition Society and the Guild and School of Handicraft in the 1880s, places to teach and exhibit traditional crafts. The British craze for handmade objects soon went global.

The Mingei Movement *1920s*

Influenced by the British Arts and Crafts Movement, Japanese art critic Sōetsu Yanagi developed the concept of *mingei*, a philosophy that praised functional, everyday objects such as pottery and textiles (p.76) made according to traditional craftsmanship and using local materials. Mingei principles emphasised a connection between beauty, function and spirituality. Imperfections were treasured marks of humility, and the anonymous artisan was just as talented as any revered fine artist. The Mingei Movement became hugely popular and helped preserve techniques that may otherwise have disappeared amid mass-production and industrialisation in Japan.

Folk art enters museums *1930s*

A major shift occurred when the museum world caught folk art fever. In 1932, 'American Folk Art' opened at the Newark Museum, with curator Holger Cahill offering the first recorded definition of folk art as 'the expression of the common people'. Cahill was also the driving force behind two landmark shows at the Museum of Modern Art at the end of the decade, featuring work by the American painter Grandma Moses (p.84) for the first time, transforming her and others into 'modern' artists. France, Japan and Mexico also established institutions dedicated to folk art.

Primitivism *1900s–1940s*

Primitivism was a Western art movement crystallising around the turn of the century that idealised the perceived unspoiled, simple and 'primitive' nature of pre-industrial and tribal societies, particularly those in Africa, Asia and Oceania. Artists like Paul Gauguin, Pablo Picasso and Henri Matisse included expressive styles and motifs inspired by African masks and sculpture. This romanticism of 'other people' contributed to the idea that the 'folk' of folk art referred to non-Western cultures, often reinforcing racist stereotypes of such cultures. Primitivism is frequently conflated with 'naive art', which shares similarly 'childlike' or unpolished aesthetics. Both these terms reveal a certain arrogance, assuming that work created outside the West or by untrained artists was charmingly crude and inferior. Inspired by his contemporaries listed above, Henri Rousseau (p.74) emerged as a prominent self-taught painter of this period, known for his flattened perspectives and vibrant jungle scenes.

The birth of 'Art Brut' *1945*

In the wake of primitivism, Western artists sought to free art from conventional constraints. In 1945, French artist Jean Dubuffet coined the term Art Brut, or 'raw art', to recognise creatively potent art made by self-taught artists, children, people affected by mental health disorders and artists living in psychiatric facilities. Operating at the fringe of mainstream art, this 'raw' movement became better known in English as 'outsider art'. It includes folk artists such as Chicago janitor Henry Darger, who created hundreds of narrative drawings and paintings from his rented room, or later, visionary Leonard Knight's magnified *Salvation Mountain* (p.122).

An international, postcolonial response *1950s–1970s*

As countries from the Global South gained independence, members of these communities sought to decolonise art as well, promoting folk art as a means to reconnect with Indigenous traditions and rediscover a culture prior to colonial encounters (see Safia Farhat, p.106 and Baya, p.108). This helped shape new national identities using visual codes, patterns and techniques that were oppressed during colonial times (such as spectacular mola blouses, p.102). In recognition of an art category turned global, the Museum of International Folk Art opened in 1953 in Sante Fe, New Mexico, showcasing folk artworks from around the world.

Black American folk art gets recognised *1960s–1980s*

The Civil Rights movement in the United States created momentum to accelerate the recognition of Black folk artists, bringing works by Clementine Hunter (p.90) to the fore. In 1982, 'Black Folk Art in America 1930–1980' opened in Washington D.C. starring Bill Traylor (p.80) and Nellie Mae Rowe, charting a new history of Black American Folk Art focusing on the American South.

Folk art sells big in America *1980s–1990s*

As folk art became recognised in the mainstream, interest from commercial galleries surged. In the 1970s, there were just two commercial galleries in the States dedicated to folk art; by the mid-1990s, there were more than 100. Publications and blockbuster exhibitions broadened folk art's scholarly and mainstream appeal, and hair-raising auction bids followed. In 1984, Ammi Phillips' (p.54) portrait *Girl in a Red Dress with Cat and Dog* sold for over $1 million at auction, the first folk artwork to do so – and not the last. In 1994, the Slotin Folk Art Auction was established as a dedicated forum for buying and selling self-taught artworks.

Surveying British folk art *2014*
Very much overdue, the breakthrough exhibition 'British Folk Art' opened at Tate Britain in 2014, featuring ship figureheads, pub signs, a cockerel sculpture made of mutton bones, and felt collages from George Smart (p.56). The exhibition helped trace a lineage between the country's folk traditions and the work of major contemporary British artists like Grayson Perry and Tracey Emin, who rose to fame with painted ceramic vases and hand-stitched quilts.

Folk art in the community *2020–*
The COVID-19 pandemic changed modes of consumption, with more intent placed on local trade, slow and mindful consumerism and practices anchored in social justice. Prolonged lockdown periods pushed many to pick up or expand their creative interests, including embroidery, knitting, woodturning, painting, drawing and more. Online workshops offered virtual community spaces, and platforms like Etsy provided a way to showcase and sell works. Global face mask shortages forced people to become resourceful by stitching and decorating upcycled fabric, showing how forgotten craft techniques can be cherished in times of crisis and uncertainty.

Where can I see it?

Victoria and Albert Museum
London, UK / vam.ac.uk
While not strictly a folk art museum, the V&A features an incredible collection of decorative arts and Arts and Crafts-inspired works from Europe, Asia and beyond, including Japanese clothing accessories, South Asian window embellishments and Islamic ceramics.

Compton Verney
Warwickshire, UK / comptonverney.org.uk
Home to the largest collection of folk art in Britain with more than 1,000 objects from private collections, including animal carousels (p.66), paintings, weathervanes and trade signs, textiles and more from the 18th century onwards.

Musée des Arts Décoratifs
Paris, France / madparis.fr
One of the largest collections of European decorative and folk art, including textiles, ceramics and furniture – from 17th-century ornamental cabinets and porcelains to 20th-century Art Deco objects.

Musée du Quai Branly – Jacques Chirac
Paris, France / quaibranly.fr
A significant collection of Indigenous art and folk traditions from Africa (including Asafo flags, p.58), Asia, Oceania and the Americas, with more than 370,000 objects. The museum is a major repository of global folk art.

American Folk Art Museum
New York City, USA / folkartmuseum.org
A leading institution showcasing American folk art since 1961, featuring a permanent collection of more than 7,000 folk art items including paintings, sculptures, textiles and decorative arts from the 18th to the 21st century.

The Smithsonian Institution
Washington, D.C. / New York City, USA
americanindian.si.edu / americanart.si.edu
Under the Smithsonian Institution umbrella, the National Museum of the American Indian has an impressive collection of Native American art, while the Smithsonian American Art Museum's dedicated galleries for folk and self-taught art include American folk art pioneers such as Bill Traylor (p.80) and Clementine Hunter (p.90).

Museum of International Folk Art
Santa Fe, USA / moifa.org
A dedicated space for international folk art since 1953, with a permanent collection of objects representing more than 100 countries. The museum also displays exciting cross-context exhibitions.

Museo de Arte Popular
Mexico City, Mexico / map.cdmx.gob.mx
Founded in the 1990s to recognise Mexican crafts and artisans, the collection is devoted to Mexican folk art, including hundreds of colourful alebrijes (p.120) produced in several regions, as well as textiles and ceramics.

Mingei-kan

Tokyo, Japan / mingeikan.or.jp

Founded in 1936 by critic Sōetsu Yanagi, who inspired the Mingei Movement, the Mingei-kan (Museum of Folk Art) includes handwoven kimonos, lacquered utensils, traditional East Asian pottery and Japanese folk paintings.

National Museum of Australia and National Gallery of Australia

Canberra, Australia / australian.museum / nga.gov.au

Indigenous and settler folk art from Australia, including textiles, ceramics and ceremonial objects from their First Nations and Torres Strait Islander collection. The National Gallery of Australia shows work by Emily Kame Kngwarreye (p.128).

African souks and craft markets

A significant amount of African folk art has been poached for the collections of Western museums. However, ceramics, tapestry, baskets, costumes, jewellery, masks and other ornamental objects can be found in the souks and markets of many towns and cities across Africa.

Contributors

Farah Abdessamad is a French-Tunisian writer. She writes about arts and culture with an interest in memory, place and expansive genealogies for publications including the *Observer*, *Art Review*, *Middle East Eye*, *The Nation*, *The Atlantic* and others.

Hoxton Mini Press is a small independent publisher from east London. We believe in books. We believe in beautiful books. We believe in beautiful books that you collect and put on nice wooden shelves and keep for future generations. We also plant loads of trees.

About the series

In an age when everything can be researched online we believe that strong opinion is better than more information. The intention of these 'opinionated' guides is not to tell you everything but to spark curiosity in the subject and, just maybe, lift your day a little. Other titles in the series include *British Art*, *Photography*, *Women Painters* and *Erotic Art*.

Artworks

Animal Figurine, c. 1981–1640 BCE

A sculpture to protect laypeople in death

You might wonder why a simple animal figurine shaped by anonymous hands more than 3,500 years ago is included in this book – not least its opening. It would be easy to overlook this artefact in a museum gallery filled with more sophisticated, sizzling objects from ancient Egypt's great pharaohs and their rich graves. (The Met's unofficial mascot, a blue hippo called William, is one such example, adorning ruler Senbi's tomb.) But this lumpy ox, missing a horn, exerts an undeniable charm, representing much more than its humble appearance; it relates to the lifestyle of most ancient Egyptians and their belief systems. This artefact was shaped to tell us a story. Part of an Egyptian burial, this object would have accompanied an ordinary peasant on their journey to the netherworld, a reminder of their earthly life labouring in the fields. It is a unique perspective from 'below' that is often left out from histories of the elites, and speaks to commonfolk hopes and concerns from this life and the next.

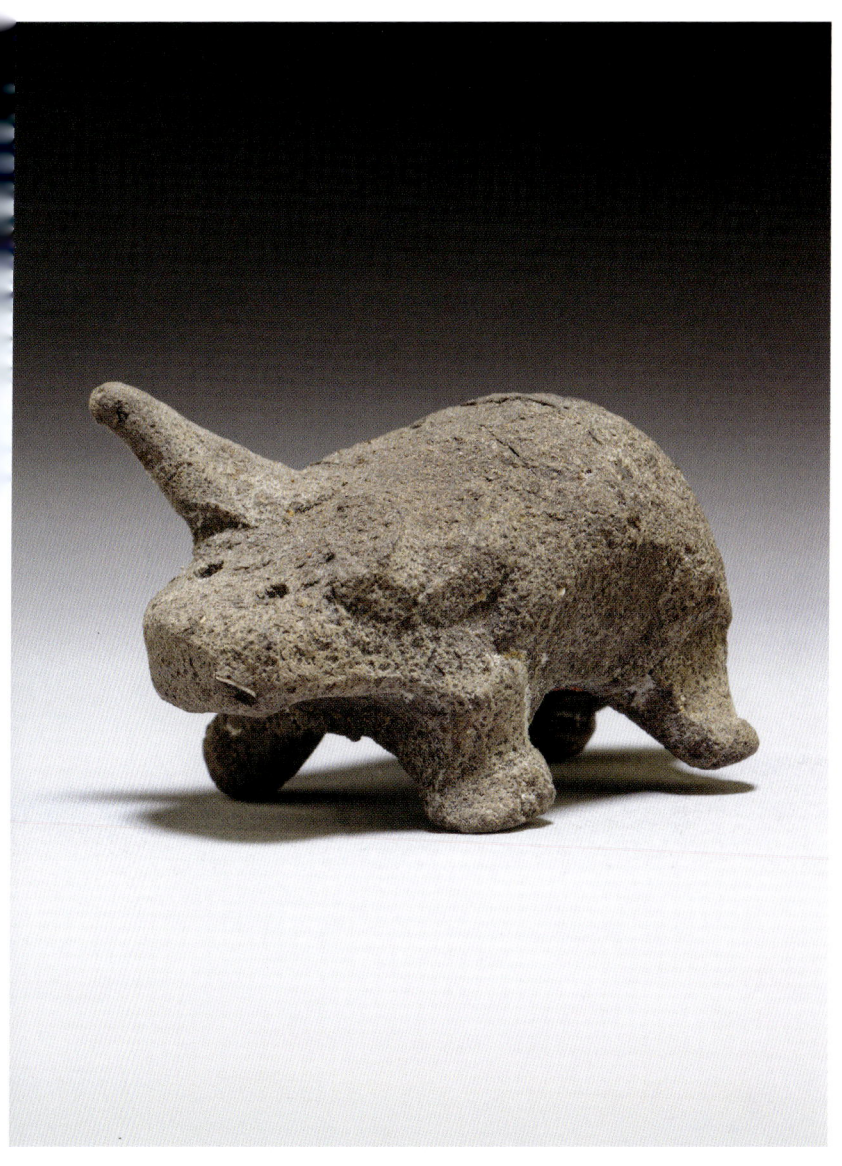

Animal Figurine, c. 1981–1640 BCE, clay, 6 × 2.9 × 3.2 cm, Metropolitan Museum of Art

Terracotta Statuette of a Siren, c. 550–500 BCE

Votive statue for a mythic monster

This ambiguous anthropomorphic object – its face bearing an enigmatic smile – is intriguing for several reasons. At first glance, the statuette's body looks like a pigeon, and its face resembles the grinning theatrical masks appearing during Greece's Archaic period (700–500 BCE). Yet it's not exactly a bird. This handmade sculpture represents one of the most feared sea creatures from the ancient Mediterranean, a siren: half-bird, half-woman. The siren's tilted head is a come-on: its presence irresistible. As told in myth, these flirtatious sirens had a destructive power, luring sailors to their deaths with charming songs (famously, Odysseus only escaped them by strapping himself to his ship's mast and instructing his crew to plug their ears with wax). Stories like these weren't just entertaining tales, but a way to warn and make sense of dangers at sea; this object might have had a votive purpose – to seek the sirens' uncertain favours and protect sailors. The myth was later repurposed in Christian art to illustrate the perils of temptation, and by the Middle Ages the siren had morphed into a more familiar watery temptress: the mermaid.

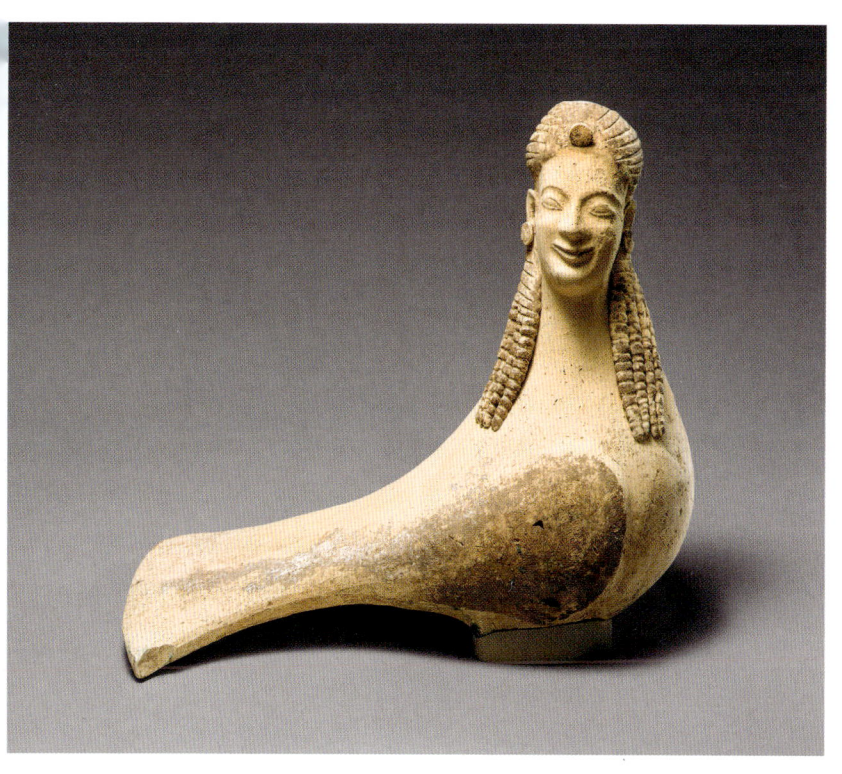

Terracotta Statuette of a Siren, c. 550–500 BCE, terracotta,
21 × 24.1 × 12.7 cm, Metropolitan Museum of Art

Shell with Inlaid Feline, c. 100 BCE–700 CE

A sacred talisman

This is our first stop in South America (there will be others), and an example of the artistic splendour of ancient Nasca culture, a pre-Inca civilisation that existed between 300 BCE and 700 CE in what is now Peru. This shell features a wild Pampas cat surrounded by vivid colour, a punch that isn't even paint: the top layer of the mollusc shell has been carefully removed, revealing a natural tangerine blush against the cat's accents of purple and pearly white. The cat itself is also made from other shell pieces, manually inserted to blend seamlessly into the surface: amazingly delicate work, considering its age. Nasca art is rife with symbols, and felines are a common motif: in 2020, a monumental cat geoglyph was discovered etched into the soil of the Nazca Desert, perhaps symbolising agricultural abundance. Eyes – appearing here on the cat's four short legs and crown – are also a frequent symbol, thought to honour the sun. This is not just a beautiful trinket, then, but likely has a ritualistic use; the two holes at the base of the shell indicate that this may have been a protective pendant, a talisman worn during special moments. The discovery of plenty of other shell necklaces suggests that they were typical garb for Nasca elites, but this one stands out for its vibrancy, complex detail and precise craftsmanship.

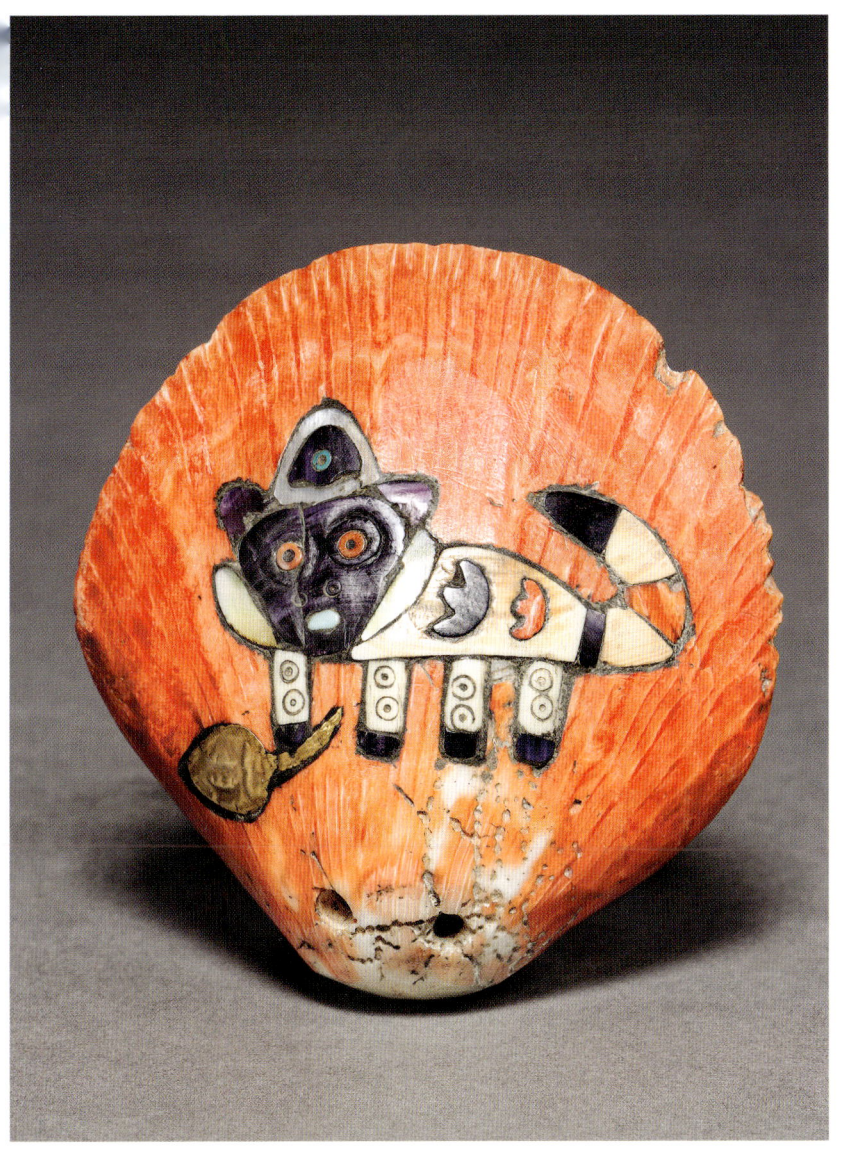

Shell with Inlaid Feline, c. 100 BCE–700 CE, spondylus shell with shell, stone and gold inlay, 7.5 × 7.4 cm, Cleveland Museum of Art

Square with a Grape Harvesting Scene, 4th–5th century

Faiths intertwined

This square of linen embroidered with wool sits at the cross-roads of several cultures. It may have existed as part of a larger piece of fabric – although only this fragment remains, making any guesses at its origin pure conjecture. Created at a time of waning polytheism in Roman Egypt, the scene of grape harvesting is significant: a popular motif in art of the period, grapes and wine were associated with long-held folk rituals and Bacchanalian feasts. But there are Christian undertones here too, the wine suggesting the blood of Christ in the Eucharist rite. All art means different things to different people, but this pastoral scene – stitched at a time of rapid cultural change – perhaps more so than most. Are we looking at the fervour of Communion, a quintessential grape harvest or simply a shared table, and a personal bond between these two neighbours, kin or friends?

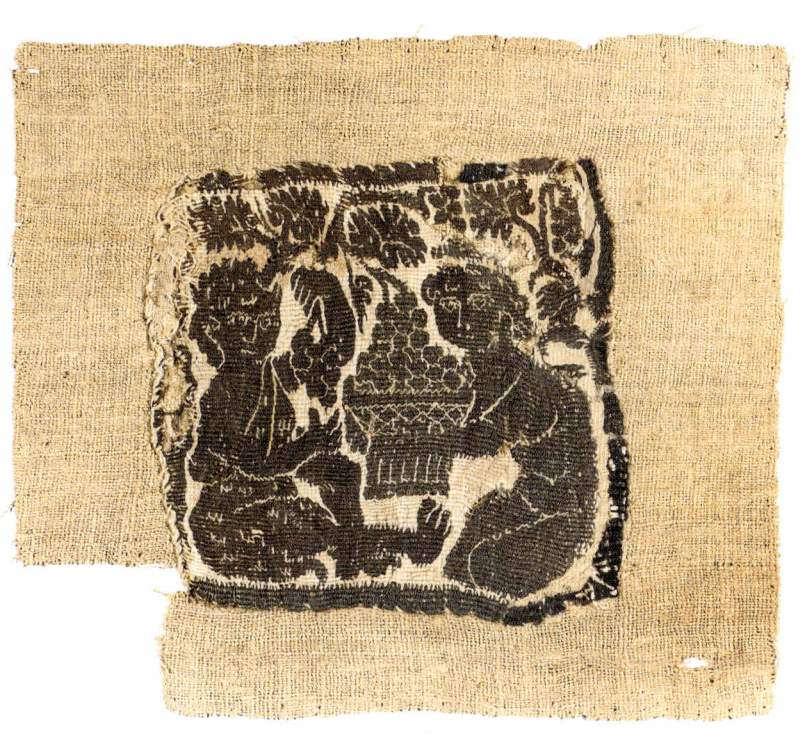

Square with a Grape Harvesting Scene, 4th–5th century, linen, wool, 14.6 × 15.4 cm, Metropolitan Museum of Art

Bottle in the Shape of a Dog, c. 1–600 CE

Bold domestic vessel

It's easy to imagine that this playful dog-shaped vessel was once someone's favourite bottle, long ago in what is now southern Peru. It's a remarkably striking object: the earthy tones beautifully contrast the animal's graphic, cookies-and-cream robe and the dog's almond eyes are adorned with black liner. This bulbous ceramic bottle could have been for daily use, decoration or ritual purposes such as burial offerings. But it wasn't a one-off; vessels such as this one were made in workshops and acquired across social backgrounds, becoming household items even for non-elites. Not only is the Nasca civilisation famous for its monumental land art, drawing enigmatic images on the desert floor, but also for its crafts, such as textiles and ceramics. As we will see across folk art – where sculptural objects sit at the intersection of beautiful, functional and homely – bottles like this often featured bold designs inspired by familiar animals and steeped in symbolism (the dog depicted here is thought to represent loyalty and companionship).

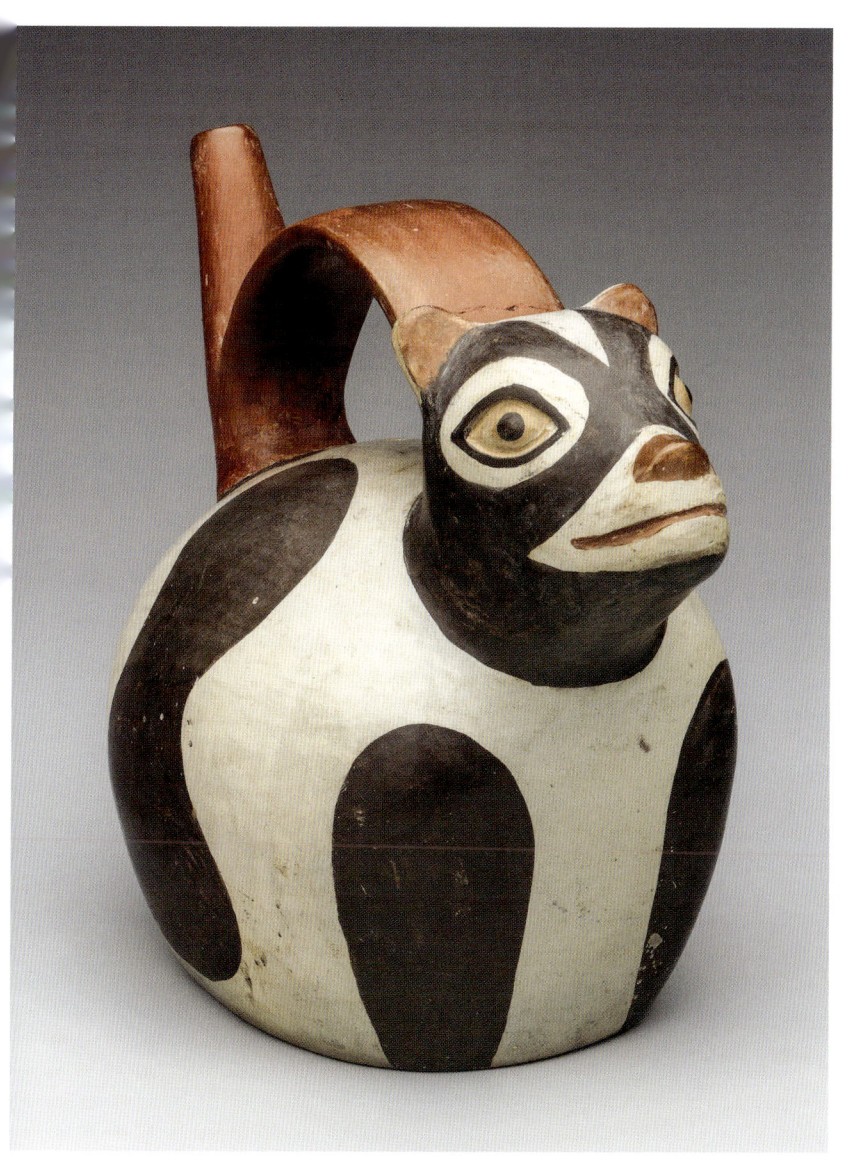

Bottle in the Shape of a Dog, c. 1–600 CE, ceramic, slip,
13 × 8.9 × 16.5 cm, Metropolitan Museum of Art

Four-Cornered Hat, c. 500–900 CE

Richly symbolic headgear

This quirky Andean head cover is more than 1,000 years old – a rather amazing fact, given its vibrant colours and impeccable condition. The pre-Inca civilisation from which it originates – either the Wari or the Tiwanaku in modern-day Peru, Bolivia and Chile – mastered sophisticated techniques. Made from soft alpaca or llama fur, it's been densely weaved, likely from the top corners down. It was created to be worn by warriors and other elite members of society and, given its phenomenal resistance to wear-and-tear, perhaps intended to be passed down between owners. Like other ancient Andean civilisations, neither the Wari nor the Tiwanaku used a writing system, so what we know about their cultures is deduced from images on artefacts like this. This hat contains a mesmerising patchwork of vignettes, including long-legged bird shapes. These are significant: Wari and Tiwanaku art is teeming with birds, from ceramics painted with abstracted wings to textile panels stitched from colourful bird feathers (a highly valued material). Birds themselves were considered divine emissaries, making this hat – plastered with religious iconography – a prized status symbol, probably donned for ceremonies including sacrificial offerings and communal feasts. (And lots of them – signs of repair and traces of hair oil found in the fabric suggest it was well-worn.)

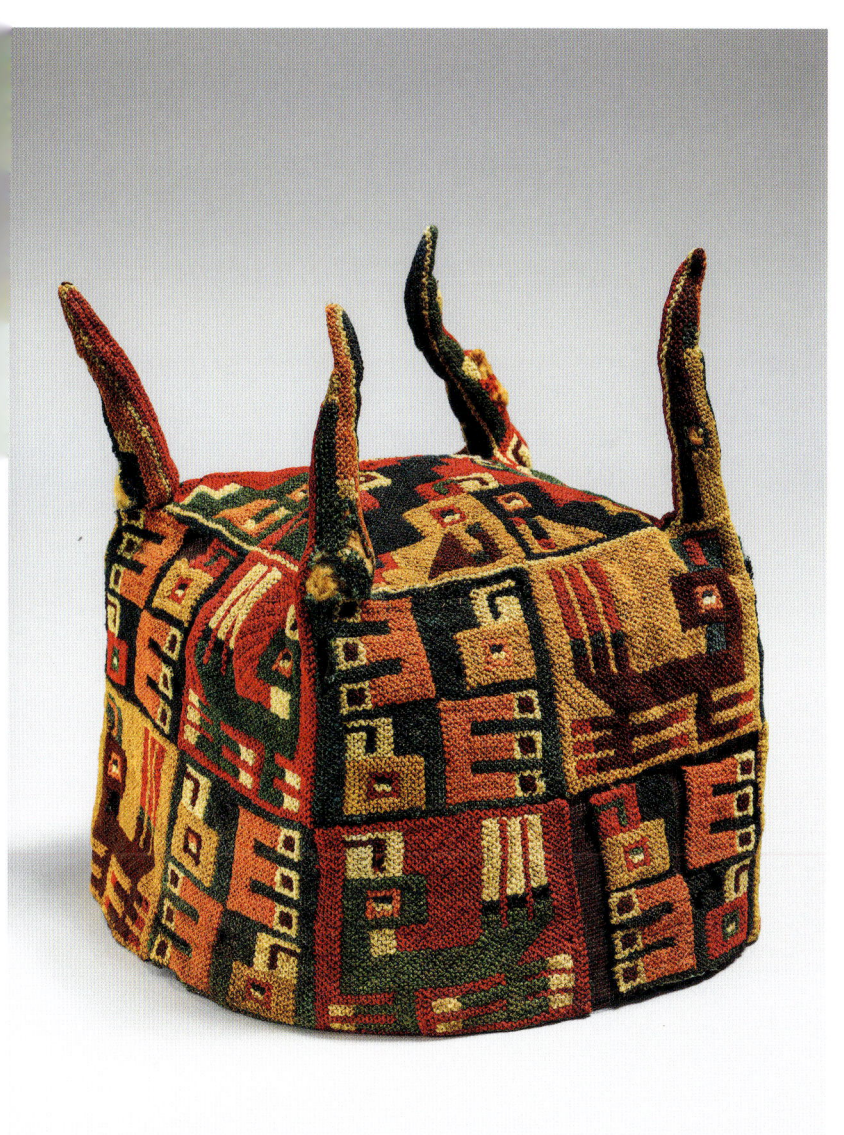

Four-Cornered Hat, c. 500–900 CE, camelid fibre, 12.4 × 17.5 cm, Metropolitan Museum of Art

Bird-Shaped Incense Burner, 12th–13th century

An ornate object for a merchant's home

In the Islamic world, burning incense is a cherished ritual. It fills interiors and streets with intoxicating scents that are believed to purify a space and repel the evil eye. Incense vessels are often heirloom treasures, and the perfect incense mix – made from wood, resins and oils – is dearly prized. This burner, with its quizzical gaze, perpendicular limbs and clawed feet, seems almost automated, as if it might creak into action at any moment. Unlike more refined palatial works of gold and silver, this one may have been purchased in a marketplace in Iran or parts of Central Asia, possibly owned by a wealthy merchant family. Birds are a significant symbol in Islam, too: the famous 12th-century Persian Sufi poet Attar of Nishapur wrote *The Conference of the Bird*, a parabolic text in which a flock of birds gather to decide which path will lead to truth, eventually steered towards God by a hoopoe. Birds were seen as trusted messengers from the sky and bearers of good news – an auspicious shape for an object that would have had pride of place in the home.

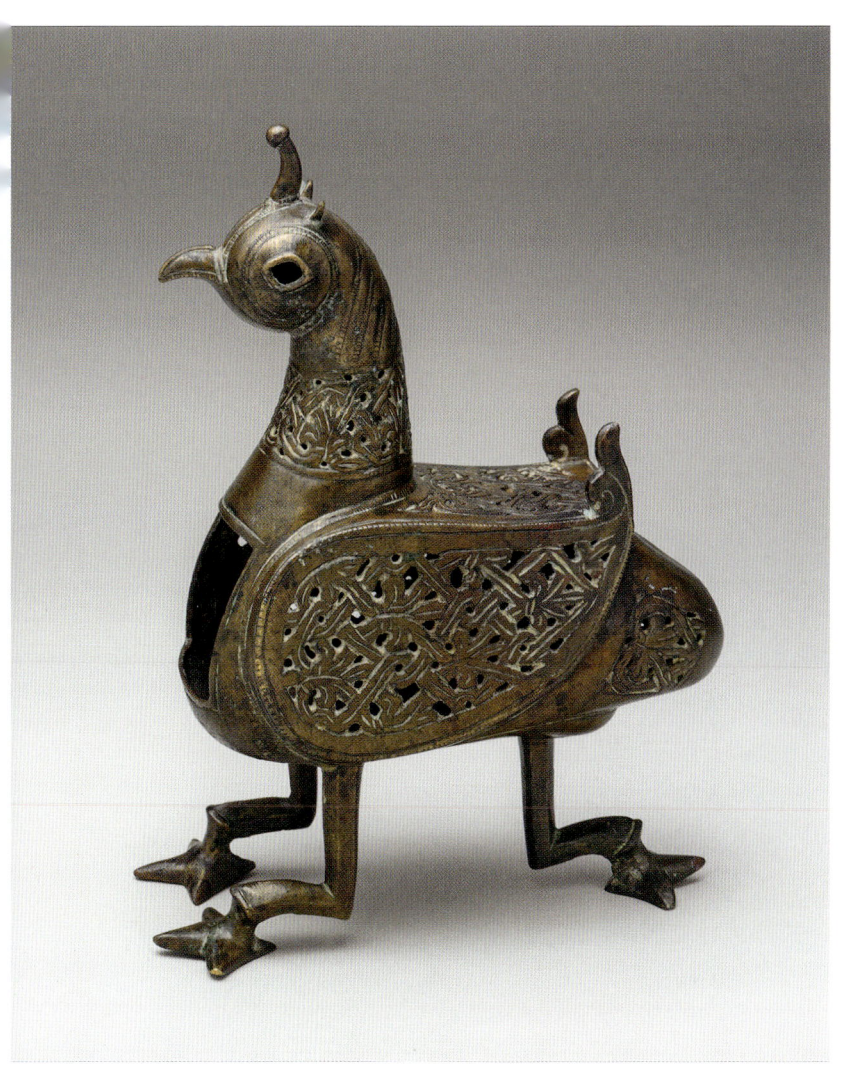

Bird-Shaped Incense Burner, 12th–13th century, bronze; cast,
pierced and engraved, 25 × 9 × 18.8 cm, Metropolitan Museum of Art

Aquamanile, c. 1200–1225

A heroic handwash

The dragon sneaks around the centaur's left flank. The centaur gathers his courage and wields his sword to slay the beast, gripping the neck of the creature in his left hand while his right mounts enough force to strike. The notion of a hero defeating a monster to save the world (or a damsel in distress) is familiar, but here it decorates a dainty hand-washing flask called an aquamanile. The detail is exquisite: his strands of hair, ornate robe and eyes of courage. It's difficult not to notice the dragon's neck appears rather erect, positioned as it is at the base of the centaur's torso; but who's to say if this is intended as a cheeky joke, or just our dirty minds jumping to conclusions. This object was created to serve a practical and social function, rather than simply for its beauty: aquamaniles were common and used for religious ablutions, their shapes emulating familiar biblical animals such as dragons and lions. But these objects are also the result of cross-cultural exchanges between the Byzantine Empire and Persia, whose sophisticated Islamic art and metalwork inspired later European artefacts.

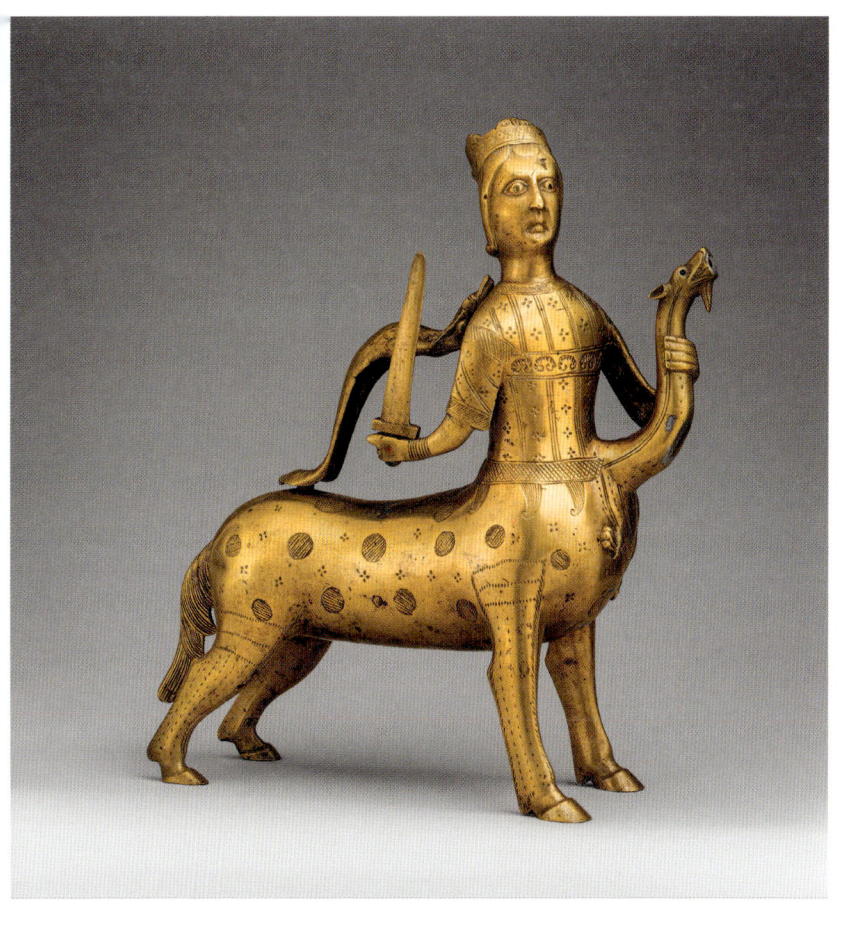

Aquamanile in the Form of a Crowned Centaur Fighting a Dragon, c. 1200–1225, copper alloy, 36.5 × 34.3 × 12.7 cm, Metropolitan Museum of Art

Tile with Women Playing a Board Game, 13th century

Everyday life captured in stone

This tile, depicting two women playing a board game on an elevated platform, is from 13th-century China. It was a turbulent era – Genghis Khan's armies tearing through Eurasia to establish the longest continuous land empire in history – and yet the scene depicted is strikingly domestic, a modest snapshot of everyday life. The women sit outside, dressed in padded clothing; presumably it's a chilly afternoon. As one woman reaches across the checkered board – which resembles the ancient Chinese game of xiangqi – to grab one of the pieces, the other woman gasps. Who lost? Did one of them cheat? Embellished tiles like this one would have adorned public spaces and interiors. Many from this period depict familiar stories and legends or illustrations of Confucian virtues and ideals, such as piety and friendship. This one stands out: its bare earthenware form, neither glazed nor painted (perhaps left unfinished), captures an endearing scene of female friendship that speaks to us to this day. What's not to love?

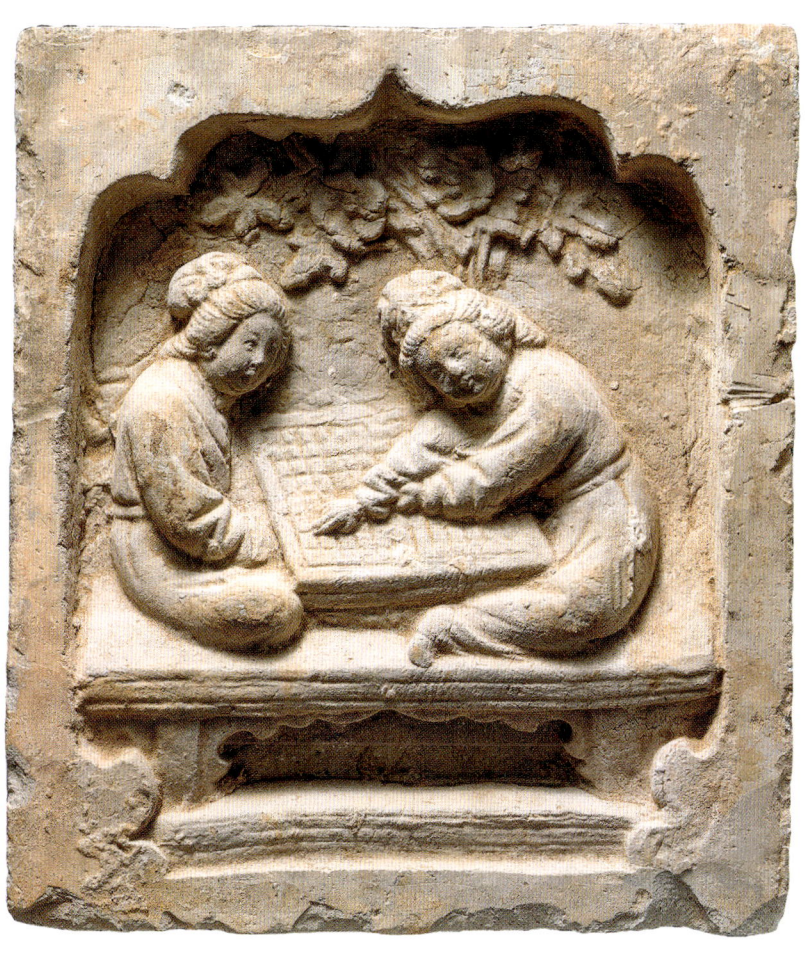

Tile with Women Playing a Board Game, 13th century, earthenware,
27.3 × 24.8 × 5.4 cm, Metropolitan Museum of Art

Box with Romance Scenes, c. 1310–1330

A box to steal one's heart

Delicately hand-carved from elephant ivory, this box from medieval France exemplifies the folk art tradition of beautifying personal containers to enhance their value. The box is decorated with tales from the Arthurian legends – medieval stories originating in Welsh and English folktales of King Arthur that were carried to the continent. The legends flourished in France especially, inspiring spin-off adventures of Lancelot, Merlin, Gawain and other Arthurian side characters. The panel depicted here is divided into two scenes: on the left, Tristan and Isolde sit around a fountain under the charm of a love potion. They only have eyes for one another; yet King Mark, Isolde's husband and Tristan's uncle, witnesses their passion. Poor guy. On the right, a man and a woman hunt a unicorn – an allegory of Christ's crucifixion. It's hard to overstate the Arthurian legends' popularity, not only recorded in prose and verse but recited, sung and performed. No doubt the owner of this box spent much time steeped in these chivalric fantasies of impossible love, virtuous sacrifices and extraordinary quests.

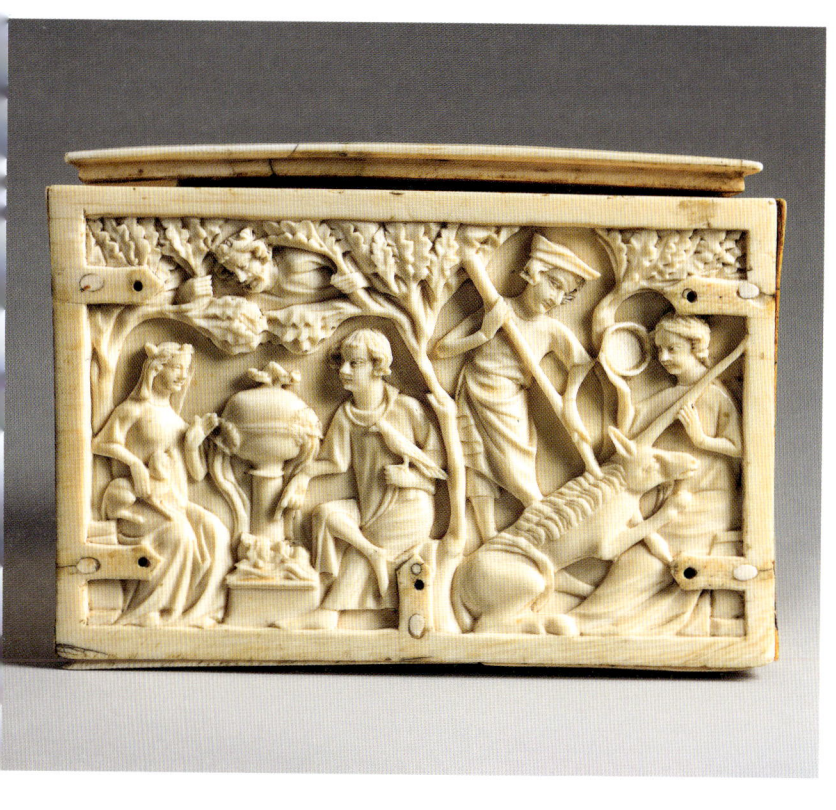

Box with Romance Scenes, c. 1310–1330, elephant ivory,
10.9 × 25.3 × 15.9 cm, Metropolitan Museum of Art

Netherlandish Proverbs, 1559

A vernacular riddle in a master's painting

In typical Bruegel fashion, there's more than meets the eye in this painting crammed with countless, haphazardly placed characters. This isn't the aftermath of a 16th-century village brawl, but a meticulously crafted record of pop cultural banter. Pieter Bruegel the Elder was hardly a self-taught, obscure artist. A master of the Northern European Renaissance, he trained with a mentor and joined painters' guilds. Yet despite this hifalutin education, he painted peasants – a rare choice, when his contemporaries chose codified biblical scenes and classical subjects. In doing so, he helped establish a genre, with rural scenes later becoming a defining motif of folk visual art. His cheeky depictions of village life offer windows into folk culture of the time: more than one hundred everyday proverbs are said to be represented in this painting alone. There's a woman putting a blue cloak on her husband (a metaphor for cheating); a couple frolicking under a broomstick (living together outside wedlock); an egg left in a nest (a reminder to always keep something in reserve). Crucially, these nuggets of vernacular speech make Bruegel's painting legible to the masses – rather than for a privileged audience – and ensure his place as one of the first artists to treat folk culture as a distinct visual genre.

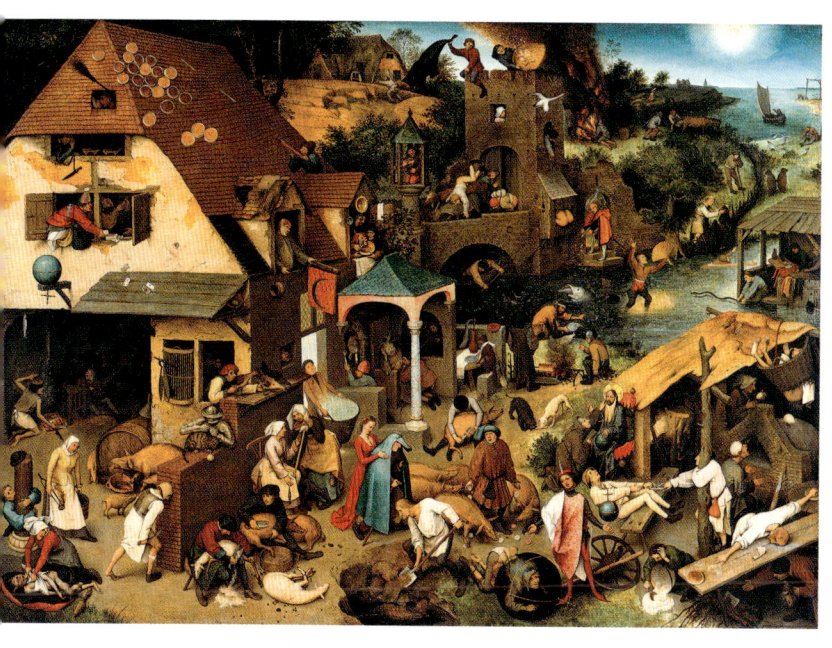

Pieter Bruegel the Elder, *Netherlandish Proverbs*, 1559, oil on oak panel,
117 × 163 cm, Gemäldegalerie, Staatliche Museen zu Berlin

A Book Peddler, c. 1670–1690

Commonfolk portrait by a mystery painter

This painting looks rather dissonant at first glance. An over-sized black hat sits heavy on the man's small frame. Together with his large brown clogs turned inwards and an uneasy posture that may suggest a disability, his appearance differs from the grand baroque portraits of 17th-century Europe, the dramatic Rubens and Caravaggios, all toned muscle and draped cloth. The man's size mimics his lower social status: he's not royalty. The humble book or gazette peddler is on the move to find clients, as his staff also suggests. This is an early example of a commonfolk portrait, where ordinary people were treated with a gravitas normally reserved for nobility. The anonymous artist, here known only by the name of their subject, borrows techniques from noble portraiture, such as showcasing the peddler's social attributes materially: muted clothing, a handful of pamphlets, a wicker basket that is perhaps carrying food, a dignified gaze directed at the viewer. This sober depiction of a salesman established a genre of folk art that would become immensely popular and prolific in later centuries, eliciting compassion and challenging what is considered worthy of being shown, acquired and collected.

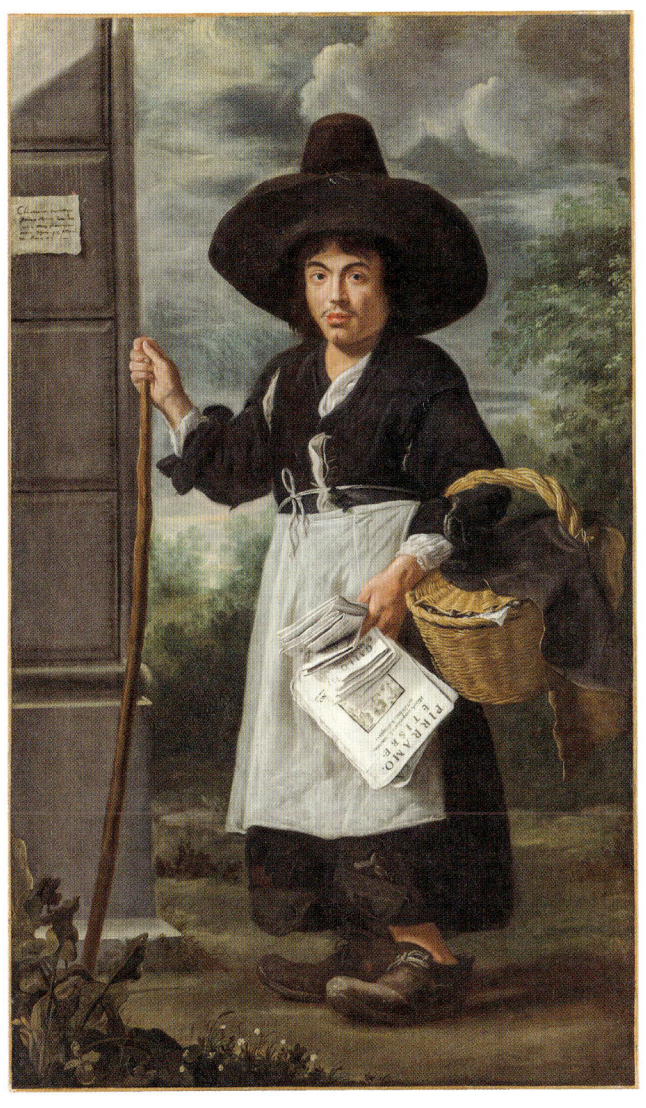

Master of the Canesso Peddler, *A Book Peddler*, c. 1670–1690,
oil on canvas, 170 × 103 cm, Metropolitan Museum of Art

Scissors Case, 17th century

A nifty symbol of devotion

This dainty scissors case, less than ten centimetres tall, sports elegant foliage, a cherub and a bird. As a token of love and fecundity, scissor sets were often included in a bride's trousseau or *necessaire* (a decorative box for pencils, tweezers and other small items). These portable objects were prized and admired, often carried in women's pockets. Scissors like these would have been used for sewing and embroidery – activities occupying many wealthy wives in their domestic lives. Made from humble steel rather than silver, this ornamental case has a dual function. Not only is it practical, protecting the scissors' sharp points, but it is carefully engraved with words in old French. Literally translating as 'by departing, my links grow', they recall the proverb that distance makes the heart grow fonder – an apt message for a wedding gift and symbol of fidelity and devotion. Key rites of passage such as betrothal and marriage were often associated with sewing and embroidery, with women spending hours tailoring dresses and stitching bridal quilts as evidence of their commitment.

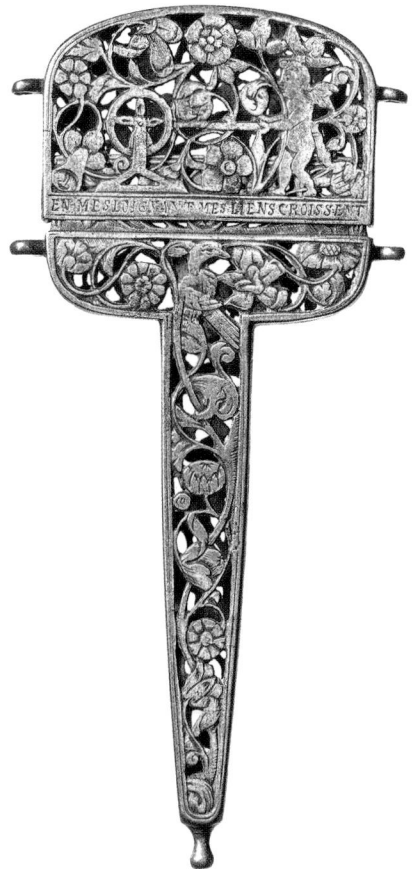

Scissors Case, 17th century, steel, 9.7 × 3.4 × 0.5 cm, Metropolitan Museum of Art

Teapot, c. 1765

An imperial relic

In many ways, British-made teapots of this period are objects of violence. In 1757, the British East India Company seized control of Bengal, cementing Britain as a major military and political power in India and sparking a growing (and aggressive) imperial interest in tea and other key commodities. Over the next century, the company came to control vast swathes of the Indian subcontinent, accounting for half of the world's trade and instigating unprecedented harm to the people of India and China – and bringing tea to the people of Britain. It was not uncommon for quirky teapots of the period to feature racist and orientalist portrayals of Asian culture. This specific teapot does not. Instead, the English rose – naively painted on each side against a crochet-like background that wraps the entire object like a doily – is evidence of tea's rapid assimilation into British culture. This quaint, charming design couldn't be more English if it tried. Even today, tea is a symbol of Britishness – and yet behind this rather banal breakfast habit is a messy, colonial history.

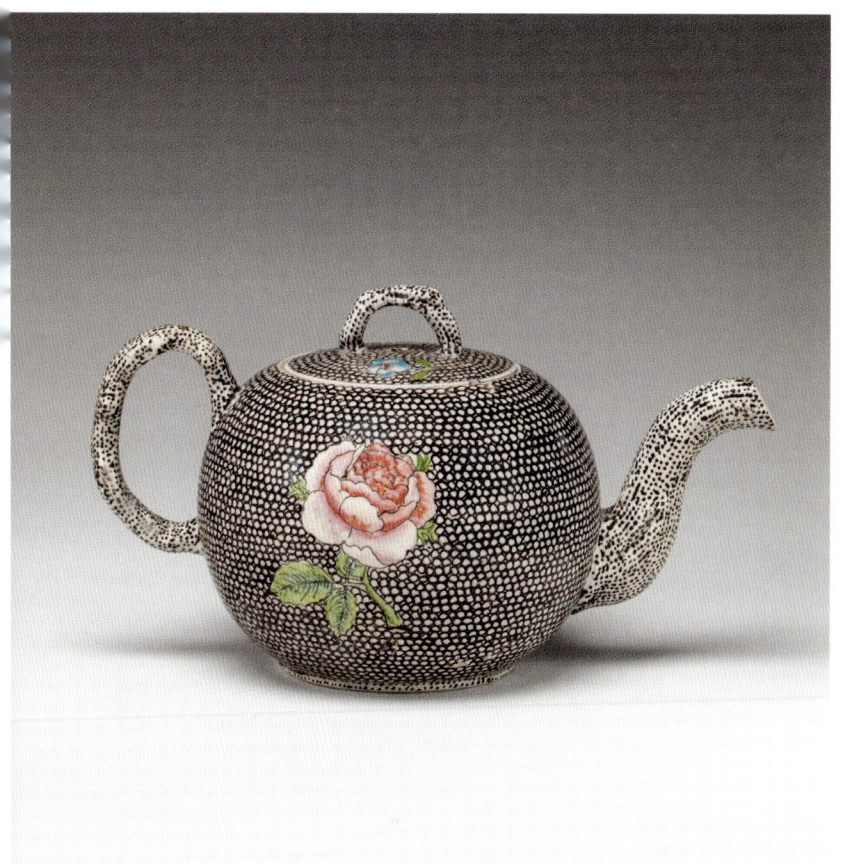

Teapot, c. 1765, salt-glazed stoneware with enamel decoration,
9.5 × 18.1 cm, Metropolitan Museum of Art

Young Woman with an Otsue Demon Dressed as an Itinerant Priest, c. 1804

A play on popular folk souvenirs

There's an air of cheeky seduction in this print. She is elegantly dressed, gushing at her suitor; he is, well, a demon disguised as a monk. It's certainly a transgressive courtship. This woodblock is an example of *ukiyo-e* art, an immensely popular genre of mass-produced paintings and prints featuring beautiful women, famous actors and erotica. But while most ukiyo-e art depicted cosmopolitan Kyoto life, this print features characters from traditional *otsu-e* folk paintings – rudimentary artworks created by artists in Otsu-Juku (a small Japanese town and popular stop along a well-trodden trade route) to satisfy tourists' demand for inexpensive portable gifts to take home. Otsu-e paintings often had a didactic moral purpose or satirical edge (the demon dressed as a monk was a common theme). Kitagawa Utamaro takes these cheeky folk characters and transports them around the world; his prints and paintings travelled far and wide, coinciding with a rising interest in *japonisme* in Europe. Utamaro's influence extended to the Impressionists, becoming a particular source of inspiration for Mary Cassatt, who adopted similar techniques of flat colour and fine lines in her own printmaking.

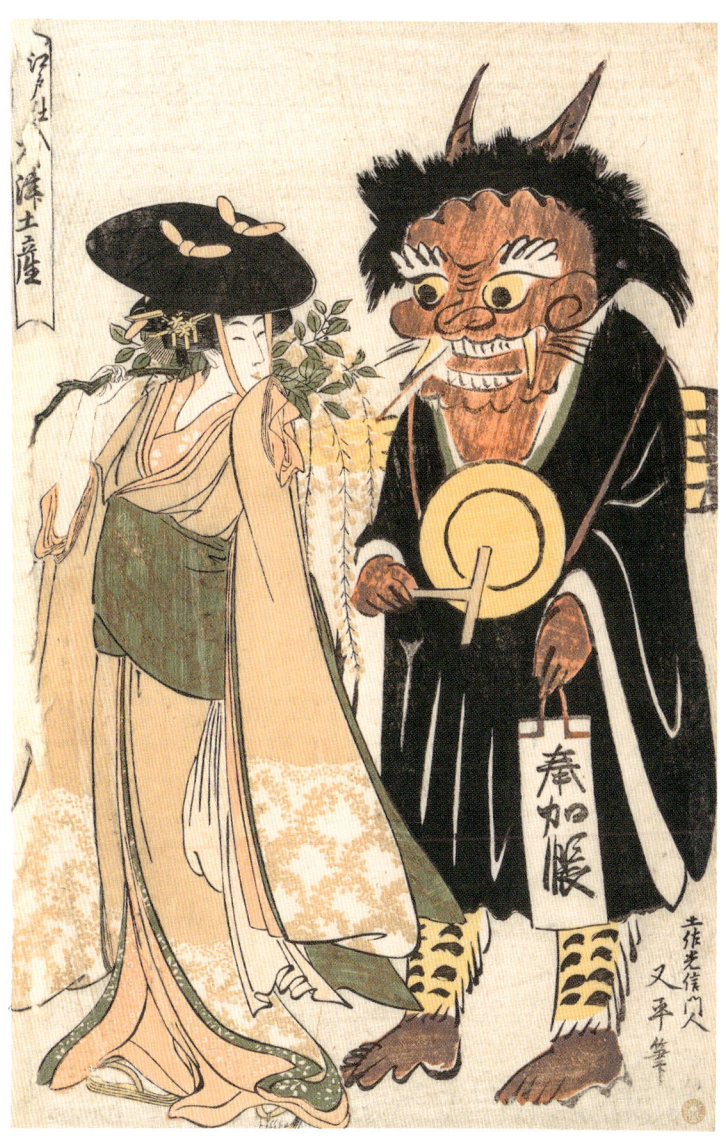

Kitagawa Utamaro, *Young Woman with an Otsue Demon Dressed as an Itinerant Priest*, c. 1804, woodblock print; ink and colour on paper, 36.8 × 24.1 cm, Metropolitan Museum of Art

Pipe Whimsy, 1809

A potter's infinite leftovers

Yes, you could smoke this pipe if you really wanted to (and no doubt some people did for good fun and special occasions). But first you might want to get lost in its hypnotic coils and admire the potter's dexterity – which was precisely the point of these puzzle pipes, or 'whimsys'. Potters from Staffordshire, a centre of British earthenware pottery from the 1700s to 1900s, were as playful as they were skilled. As early as 1750, they shaped these pipes from leftover clay at the end of their shift, challenging one another to make ever more intricate whimsys. The competitions culminated in highly impractical yet mesmerising objects. This one, with its infinity knot swirls and dainty patterns, was probably threaded with a damp string to hold the coils in place while firing. The right texture mattered immensely: too dry and it would crack, too wet and it may not hold. Tradition often credits Fenton Pottery owners Felix Edward and Richard Pratt for making the first coiled stem tobacco pipes, which were initially traded among friends but later sold, once locals caught wind of these snazzy accessories. Sometimes leftovers are the best bit.

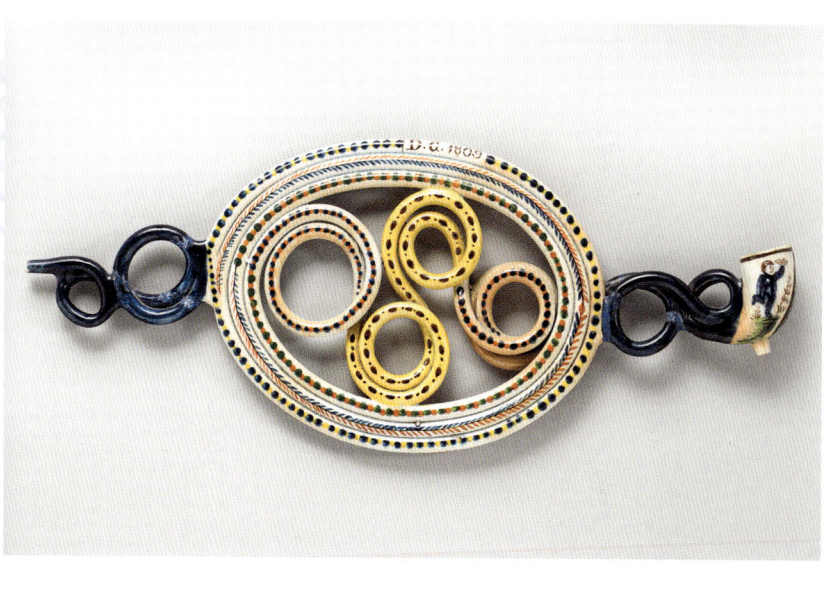

Pipe Whimsy with Figure Eights, 1809, Prattware, 14.3 × 34.6 cm, Metropolitan Museum of Art

WILLIAM MURRAY

Family Register, 1813

An intricate personal record

We're looking at Daniel Contryman's personal genealogical record, a man born in 1785 somewhere – we're not told – in the newly independent United States of America. Though it depicts the names of his family members and marriage in painstakingly symmetrical composition, this is not a legal document. It's a prized heirloom (kept in the Contryman family for 150 years before being donated to a museum) in a distinctive style: *fraktur*. Fraktur art is named after the typeface – broken, gothic lettering – which was widespread in 18th-century Germany and brought to Pennsylvania by motley groups of religious dissidents fleeing persecution in Europe. These immigrants wrote their family records in the characteristic typeface, adorning baptismal documents, birth certificates, land deeds and even bookplates with rich iconography. Traditional European fraktur (originating in Alsace, Switzerland and the Rhineland) was black and heavy, the language of dense philosophical treatises and religious manuscripts, but in the States it evolved. Artists like William Murray sought to personalise their work with ever more elaborate borders, dreamy illustrations and colour.

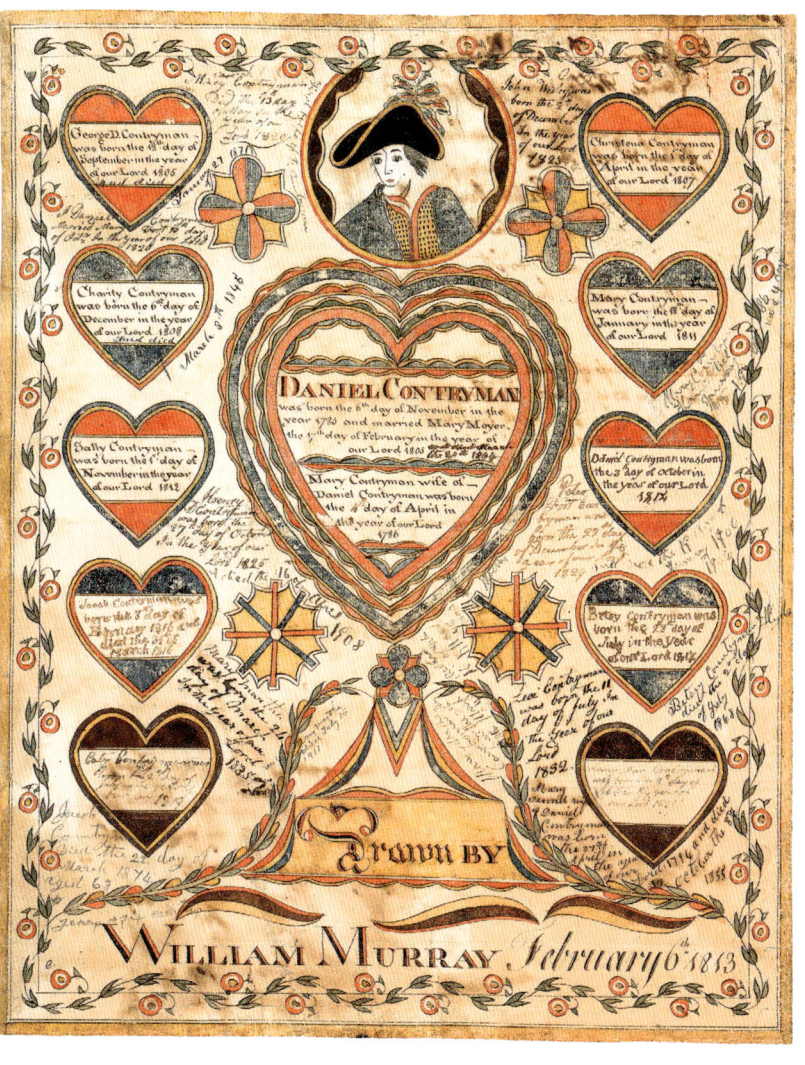

William Murray, *Family Register*, 1813, ink, pencil and pigments on paper,
39.8 × 32.5 cm, Minneapolis Institute of Art

ROSENA DISERY

Sampler, 1820

A covert expression of freedom

This extraordinary document is one of only two samplers recovered from New York's African Free School, an institution established in 1787 in Lower Manhattan that provided education to formerly enslaved Black people as well as those born free. In America as well as in Europe, samplers were prized evidence of a young woman's mastery of needlecraft. As a token of graduation, they included various letters, numbers and shapes that demonstrated years of applied practice. Because they acknowledged individual achievements, samplers were commonly signed and dated, and thanks to such details, we know that Rosena Disery was a young Black American. Although Disery was born free, under New York's Gradual Abolition Law she would have needed to wait to be fully recognised as such, since slaveowners were still entitled to her service up to 1827. This context is important: surrounded by innocuous floral imagery, the sampler bears an abolitionist message. The stanza that Disery reproduced comes from a poem disseminated in English and American anti-slavery circles. The search for truth takes on a poignant meaning in the context of a long and painful road towards Black emancipation.

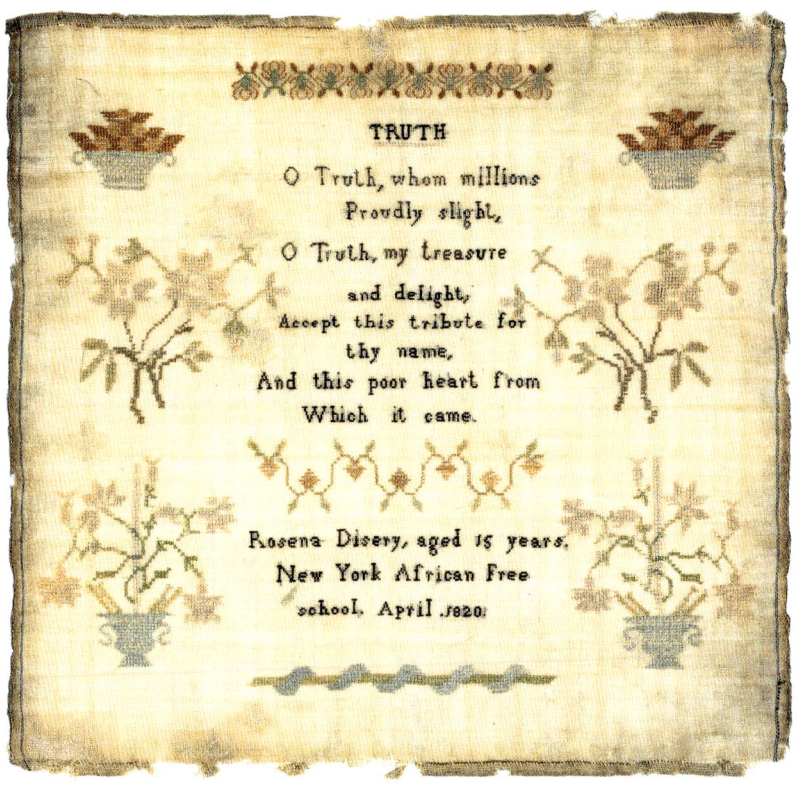

TRUTH

O Truth, whom millions
Proudly slight,
O Truth, my treasure
and delight,
Accept this tribute for
thy name,
And this poor heart from
Which it came.

Rosena Disery, aged 15 years,
New York African Free
school. April .1820.

Rosena Disery, *Sampler made at the New York African Free School*, 1820,
silk on wool, 30.5 × 33 cm, New York Historical Society Museum and Library

Girl in a Red Dress, c. 1835

Painting on the road

This great work of American folk art is all in the details: the girl's concentrated expression, the red accessories matching her puff-sleeved dress, her rosy cheeks. Ammi Phillips was a popular self-taught itinerant artist working across the East Coast, earning his living through producing more than 500 portraits in his lifetime. With the new medium of photography reserved for the elite few who could afford it, Phillips' work catered to the provincial middle class keen to portray – and aggrandise – their social status. He devised a remarkably successful template for portrait painting, pairing his model with personalised touches – here, ripe strawberries and a coral necklace to ward off bad luck. There are several versions of Phillips' *Girl in a Red Dress*, which likely featured different models, including one with a cat and a dog (becoming the first folk artwork to sell for more than $1 million at auction in the 1980s). But the red-on-red of the girl's dress, shoes, flushed cheeks and the single strawberry stem make this version especially daring and playful. Capturing an age of innocence, we are drawn to this scarlet revelry and the two pairs of eyes – the girl's quizzical gaze and the puppy's big, round, tender stare, faithfully by her side.

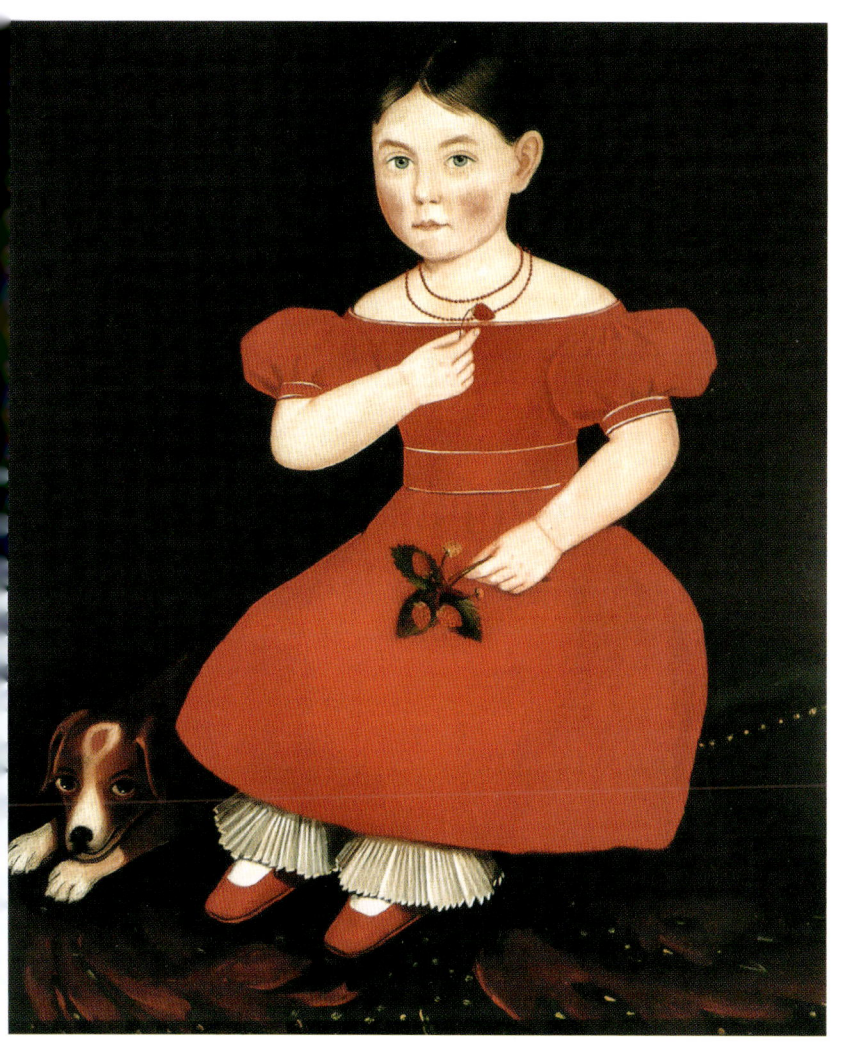

Ammi Phillips, *Girl in a Red Dress*, c.1835, oil on canvas,
82.2 × 69.5 cm, Terra Foundation for American Art

Old Bright, the Postman, c. 1840

Portrait of a local icon

This is the story of an obscure East Sussex folk artist gaining major institutional recognition more than a century after his death. George Smart, a tailor by trade, chronicled daily life and local figures in and around his village of Frant in mixed-media collages created from scraps of cloth left over from his day job. Here, the postman – nicknamed Old Bright – and his donkey, cut from felt and laid against a peachy watercolour background, are on their way to Frant. Just one more mile, according to the milestone. The postman has a hunched back and cold-bit cheeks: it's a taxing journey. Old Bright was one of two quirky characters Smart returned to regularly, producing several versions of this piece. Not much is known about Smart's life, though references to his shop in contemporaneous guidebooks tell us that these portraits were probably souvenirs. His body of work remained largely scattered and unknown until 2014, when 21 of his collages were included in a major exhibition at Tate Britain, catapulting Smart into renown and ensuring his place as one of the key figures in English folk art.

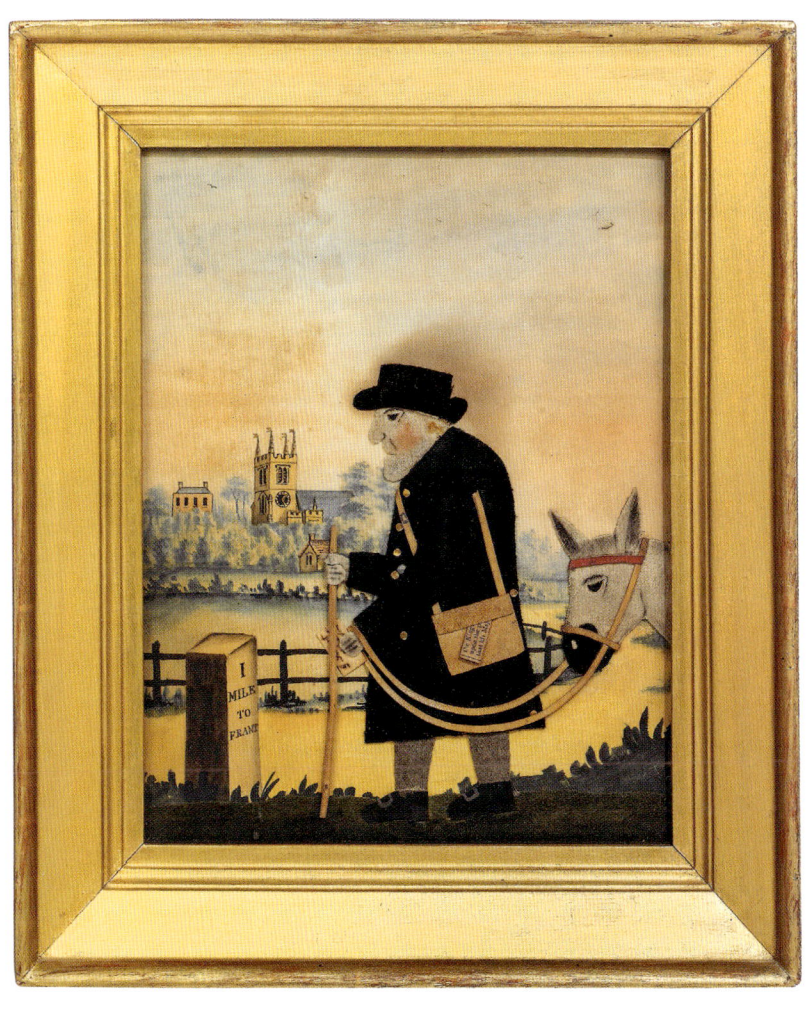

George Smart, *Old Bright, the Postman, Leading a Donkey,*
with Frant Church in the Distance, c.1840, cut felt, 26.7 × 21 cm, private collection

Asafo Flag, c. 1863

Coded signal of strength

In the 1800s, the coastline of today's Ghana was a hotly con-
tested region, prized for its commodities including precious
metal, cocoa and enslaved people. With these appetites came
tentative alliances: the British, who had wrestled control from
the Dutch, struck up a deal with the native Fante people,
relying on their warrior groups – known as Asafo – as extra
manpower. This is an Asafo battle flag, an important aspect
of how an Asafo company conveyed its pride and identity.
The flags often represented visual idioms of power and unity,
and this one is evidence of the delicate relationship the Fante's
Asafo had with their colonisers. Eight people reel in a net that
has captured a large fish – a symbolic expression of strength
in numbers. The Union Jack in the top left speaks to their
allegiance to the British, but the message here is clear: Asafo
companies could come together to trap and take control of
a European fort just as easily as the fish. Watch your back, it
says; the Fante should not be underestimated.

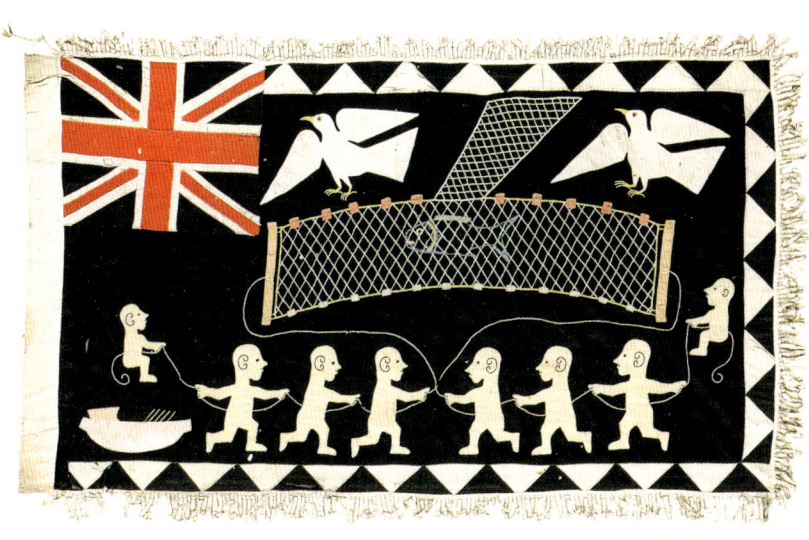

Asafo Flag, c. 1863, appliqué and embroidered cloth,
114.3 × 186.7 cm, Detroit Institute of Arts Museum

ISRAEL DOV ROSENBAUM

Mizrah, 1877

Papercut to guide prayers

Mizrah is the Hebrew word for 'east' as well as the name
of these decorative plaques. European Jews living west of
Israel would hang mizrahs on an eastern wall of their home
to direct their prayers towards Jerusalem's destroyed temple.
This one is a papercut, a wonder of symmetry and intricate
minutiae. The grand temple is surrounded by lions, deer,
roosters, snakes, oxen and more – a delicate menagerie, full of
symbolism. The lions are especially significant: an emblem of
the tribe of Judah and a sign of strength. And it was needed.
This mizrah, handcrafted by Israel Dov Rosenbaum, was
given to his daughter Bessie at a time when the increasing
persecution of Jews in Eastern Europe sent family members
fleeing in different directions. In this context, the mizrah
takes on a new significance, an object to orient Jews towards
their spiritual centre. The practice of praying towards a
mizrah could have disappeared during the Holocaust, but
was revived by survivors and their descendants, and remains
an important religious touchstone for diasporic Jews today.
We're admiring a sacred image: a holy temple that survives
on paper and in hearts.

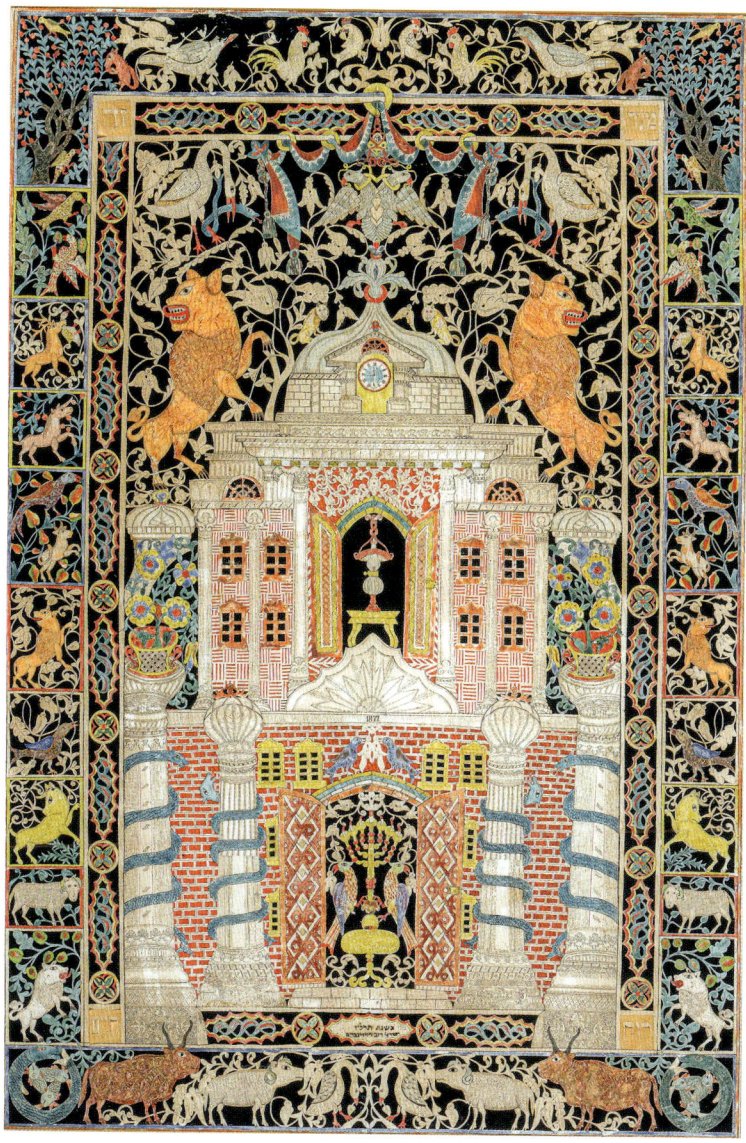

Israel Dov Rosenbaum, *Mizrah*, 1877, paint, ink and graphite on cut-out paper, 77.5 × 53.5 cm, Jewish Museum, New York

Shield, c. 1885

A Sioux warrior-artist and his thunderbird

In Native American mythology, the thunderbird is a powerful spirit that can control the weather, creating storm clouds, rain showers and slices of lightning. Its prey: white American settlers who, during the 19th century, extended their colonial reach westward to the Great Plains, believing it was their 'manifest destiny' to spread capitalism across North America and displacing and subjugating Indigenous peoples in their wake. This shield belonged to Sioux artist Joseph No Two Horns, who fought in numerous battles alongside other Plains tribes against the settlers, famously defeating the US Army at the Battle of Little Bighorn in 1876. The shield has obvious physical protective properties, but the thunderbird is an apt choice of decoration, a spirit animal that provides strength and guardianship. Joseph No Two Horns was not just a warrior; he was also an artist. He chose to paint his thunderbird on buffalo hide. Traditionally used for shield-making, this was an increasingly rare material in the late-1800s as settlers tactically hunted the animals to near extinction. The result is a symbol of Native American pride and defiance.

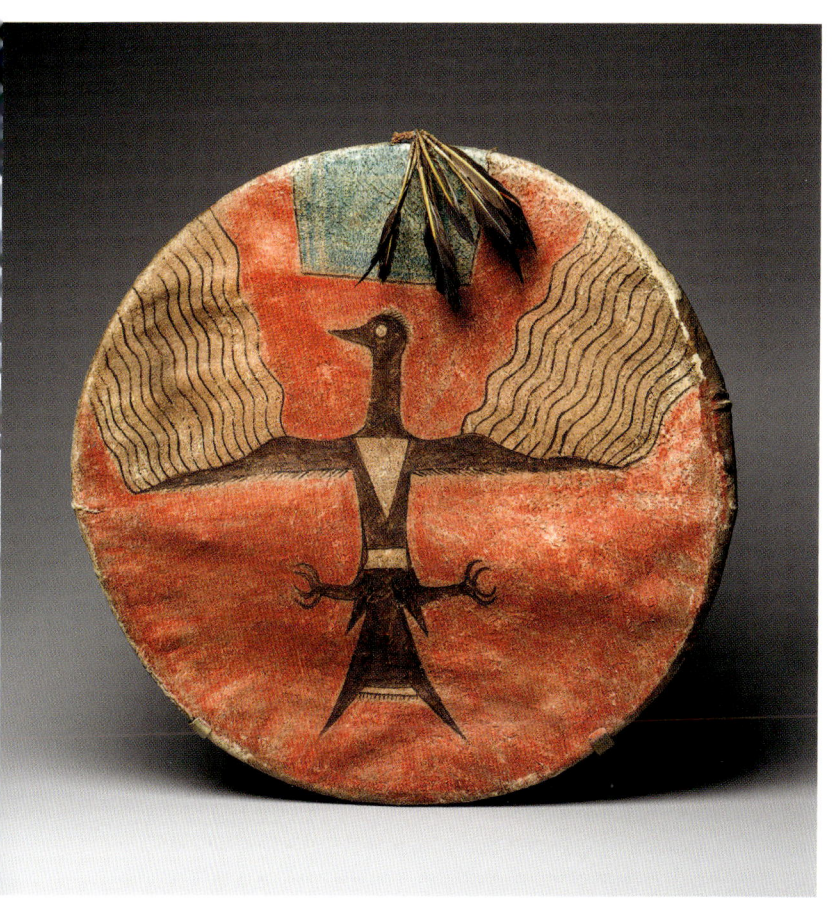

He Nupa Wanica / Joseph No Two Horns, *Shield*, c. 1885, tanned leather, pigment, wood and feathers, 1.6 × 41.9 cm, Metropolitan Museum of Art

Bible Quilt, c. 1886

Stitching stories within stories

Born into slavery in Georgia, self-taught textile artist Harriet Powers was a pioneer figure in the great American folk art tradition of quilt-making. Powers' letters mention several quilts, and it's thought that post-emancipation she supported herself as a seamstress, but only two of these works are known to survive. This one depicts 11 biblical scenes in graphic cotton appliqué vignettes (where pieces of fabric are cut out and stitched onto another, larger piece). The scenes – separated by lines reminiscent of farm field borders – are arranged linearly. In the top left we see Adam and Eve in the Garden of Eden, a serpent curving towards them; in the bottom right, the Last Supper and Holy Family. The middle panel includes a portrayal of Jacob's ladder – an Old Testament story popular among enslaved people, who interpreted the stairway to heaven as an escape from bondage. Field songs sung by enslaved people were often rooted in biblical stories, and this songcraft became a way of expressing the extreme suffering they endured at the hands of white enslavers. Infused with these Black folk traditions, Powers' quilt is coded with messages of loss and freedom, longing and possibility.

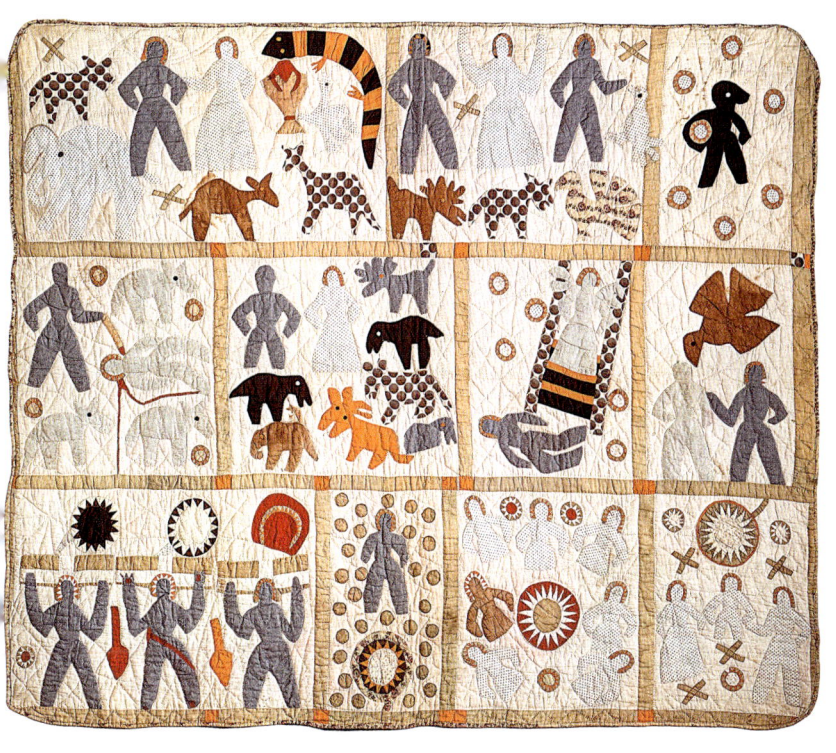

Harriet Powers, *Bible Quilt*, c. 1886, cotton, 191 × 227 cm, Smithsonian

Fairground Carousel Pig, c. 1850–1900

Farmyard entertainment

Carousels date back to medieval times – although then they were used as training grounds for soldiers who swung lances and swords, and practised ball throwing on moving objects. Indeed, the name originates from the Italian and Spanish *carosella*, or 'little war', used to describe a combat exercise played among 12th-century horsemen. The ride evolved over time, swapping real and wooden horses for increasingly exotic animals, from camels and peacocks to sea monsters, and operating techniques became more mechanised. The first steam-powered carousel was introduced in England in 1861, coinciding with the increasing popularity of Victorian funfairs as amusement grounds for bedazzled children and families, newly flush with disposable income and precious leisure time. Far from the kind of fearsome animal you'd steer into battle, this plump pig – with its understated palette and elegant leap – is also notably less garish than the carousel animals of today. It's a window into an era when candy floss and hook-a-duck formed the golden age of entertainment, a time when a humble pig could be as fancy as a stallion.

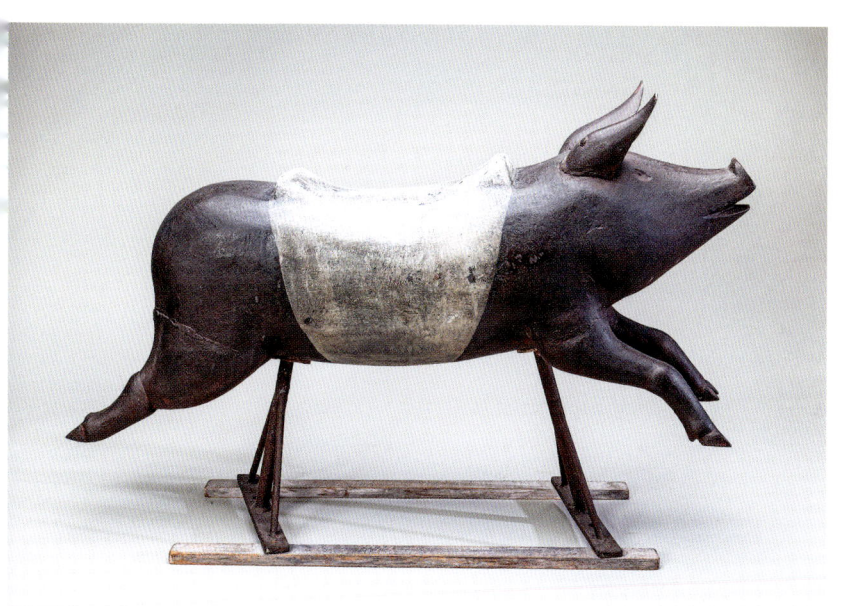

Fairground Carousel Pig, c. 1850–1900, cast iron, 79 cm high, Compton Verney

UNKNOWN ARTIST

Cradleboard, c. 1890

Baby on board

This cradleboard is from the Ute tribe, indigenous to Utah (the state is named after them), Colorado and New Mexico. Cradleboards have traditionally been used as portable carriers for infants across many Native American tribes, as well as in Central Asia, and are still used by some communities today. The baby is held in place within the leather attached to the arched wooden backboard, while the headpiece shields them from the sun as their kin go about their day. Folk art regularly blurs the boundary between functional and artistic objects, and this cradleboard is no exception. Glass beads painstakingly stitched into intricate patterns express the visual identity of the tribe, and the yellow-ochre colour signals that this cradle was for a baby girl (white clay paint was used for boys). She was protected, not just by the wooden panel and inside padding, but also by dangling amulets. Often animal-shaped, these sometimes held part of the baby's umbilical cord for an additional layer of spiritual companionship.

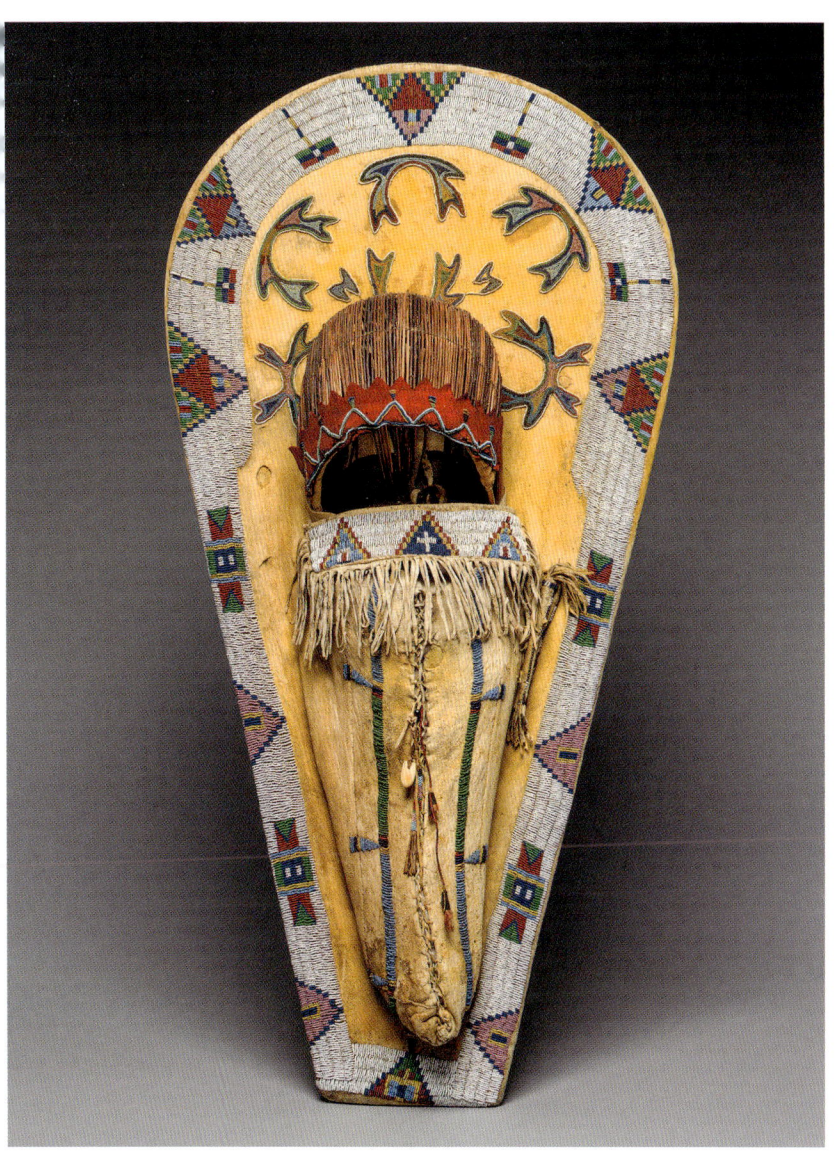

Cradleboard, c. 1890, wood, tanned leather, pigment, glass beads, wool cloth, metal cones, feathers and bone, 102.9 × 52.7 × 17 cm, Metropolitan Museum of Art

Violin Case, 1891

Homage to multiple American identities

Dated only two years after the establishment of the Brulé
Lakota Rosebud Reservation in South Dakota where it was
obtained, the only clue we have to this violin's ownership
are the mysterious initials on its case. 'R.B.' could have been
a member of the Rosebud Sioux Tribe who live on the reservation – missionaries recruited Native American children
into schools where they would have been introduced to the
instrument. (This was how famous violinist and Sioux activ-
ist Zitkala-Ša first learned to play.) Or perhaps 'R.B.' was a
white settler who commissioned a Native American artist to
decorate the case with elaborate beadwork – an important
part of Native American culture. Since the 16th century, these
communities incorporated European glass and ceramic beads
into their traditional designs and stitching patterns. Here,
Indigenous symbols (such as the diamond shape associated
with medicine men and sometimes used to represent a tipi) are
paired with the familiar stars-and-stripes flag and Christian
crosses. It's a strikingly cross-cultural object that speaks to
complex questions of statehood and identity formation amid
the tribe's loss of ancestral territory.

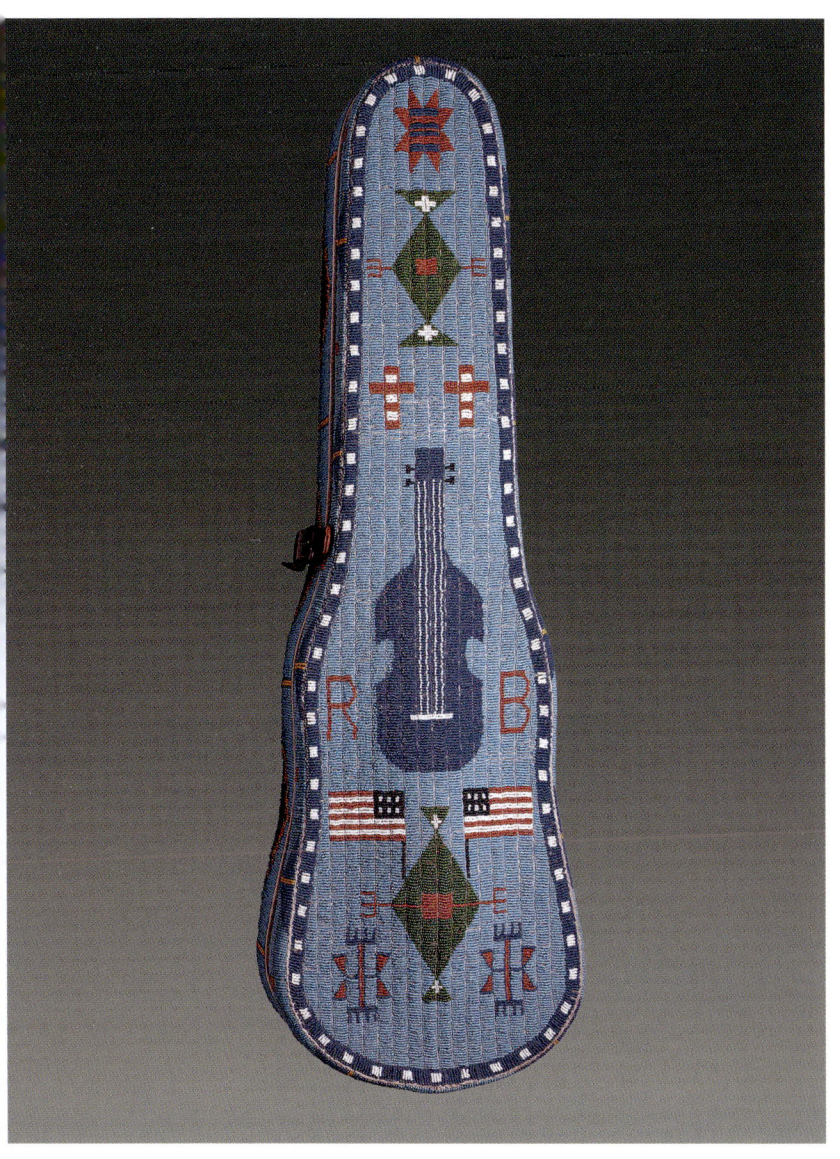

Violin Case, 1891, glass beads, commercial wood case, native-tanned hide, metal trim, 81.3 × 25.4 × 11.4 cm, private collection

Hay Cutting, c. 1907

A Russian hay day

This is the work of Russian avant-garde extraordinaire Natalia Goncharova. She was a member of the most daring creative movements of the time, including becoming an unforgettable émigré costume-designer in the extravagant Ballet Russes during the interwar years in Paris. So why is such a well-connected, glamorous artist in this book? Goncharova straddled two worlds. She exhibited with major Russian art salons, but she was continually fascinated with the country's folk culture, which appears again and again in her work in the form of peasant labourers, legendary heroes and agrarian landscapes, pioneering a revival of folk motifs which made her famous during her lifetime. Goncharova's early paintings bear the hallmarks of primitivism: this rustic scene, with its cartoonish rendering and punchy colour, is likely influenced by *lubki*, Russian woodcut prints. Lubki traditionally depicted saints and religious icons, but Goncharova's painting centres on the good people of the Russian countryside, feeding the country. This was a time of political and cultural upheaval, and Goncharova was at the helm. Old Russia meets the dawn of a New Russia, with its tentative promise of freedom through exalted labour and collective agency.

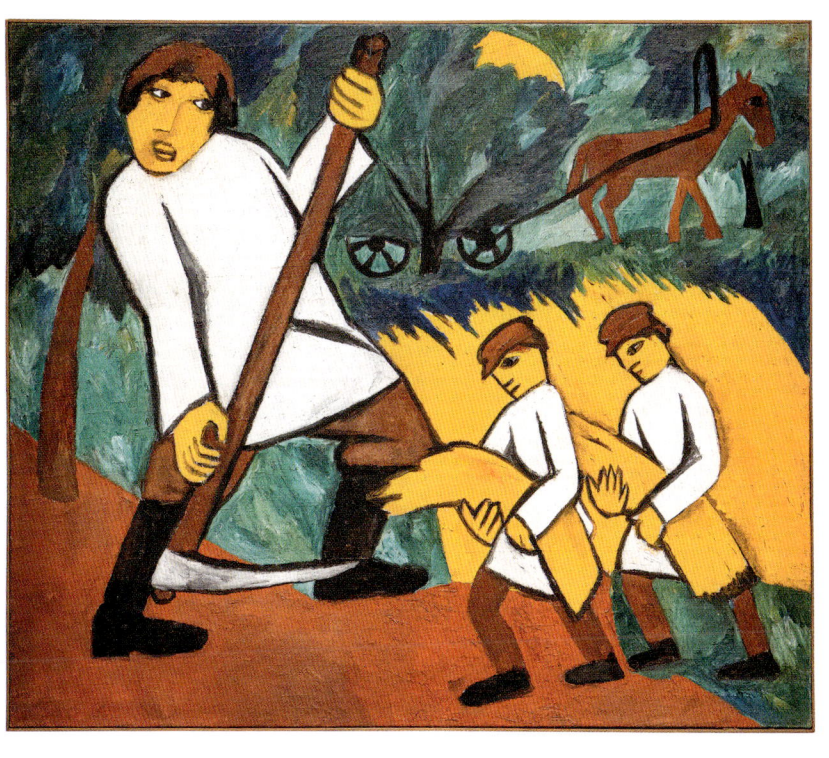

Natalia Goncharova, *Hay Cutting*, c. 1907, oil on canvas,
98 × 118 cm, Galerie Gmurzynska, Cologne

The Football Players, 1908

Modern life captured with joy

He's the folk artist for whom Picasso threw a drunken banquet in Paris, the same year this painting was completed. Nicknamed the *douanier* (customs officer) for his day job as a tax collector, Henri Rousseau was at the forefront of 'naive art' – a movement characterised by its simple, unaffected style. Though Rousseau was ridiculed by Academy critics, Picasso took pride in having 'discovered' him, introducing him to the wider circle of Montmartre bohemians, who fawned over the douanier's primitivist style. Here, four men play a ball game – not football, contrary to the title, but rugby, commemorating the first international game between France and England. It's an undeniably bizarre scene. The players look rather quirky, with their twinned outfits, exaggerated movements and similar features; the trees are oddly small and the clouds look like solid objects. It's easy to see why his flat, non-naturalistic perspective charmed the Avant-Garde. Rousseau made his name with his lush jungle landscapes, but *The Football Players* best demonstrates the childlike qualities that many adulated in him as an outsider artist.

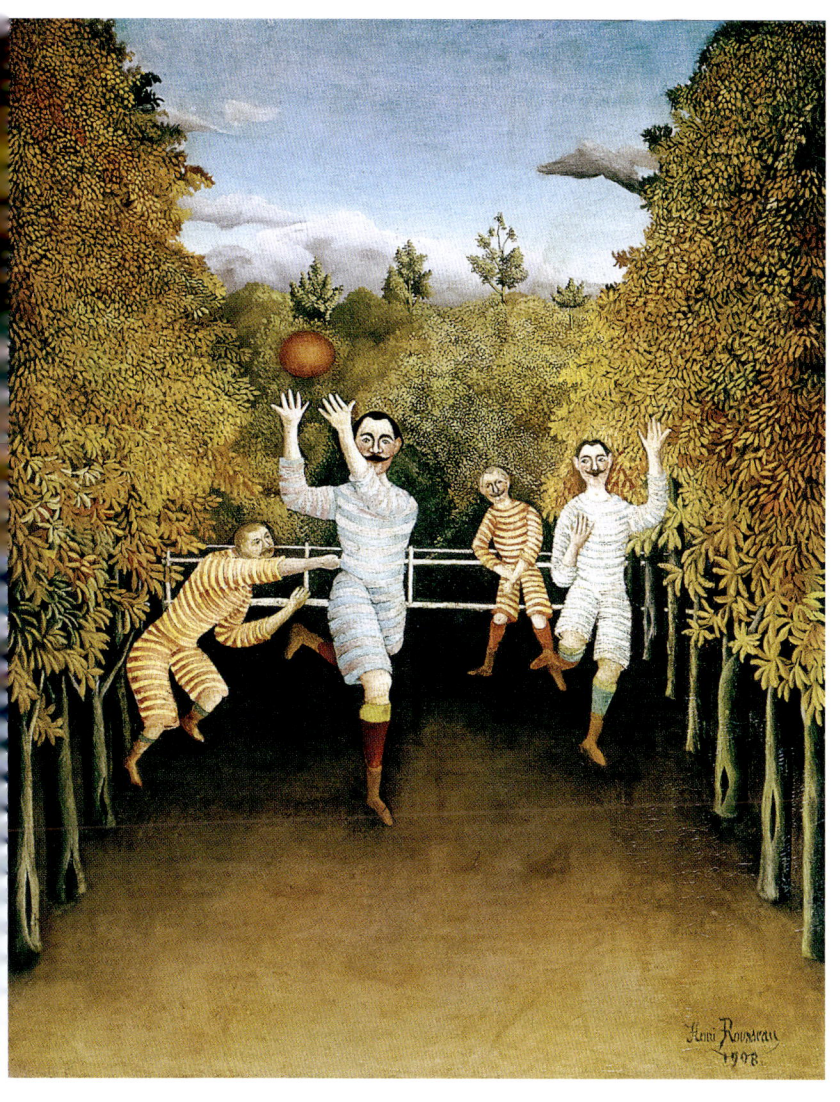

Henri Rousseau, *The Football Players*, 1908, oil on canvas,
100.3 × 80.3 cm, Guggenheim New York

Farmer's Coat, 1920

Beauty in imperfection

Stitched from cotton scraps, this coat is not just the product of necessity but an expression of a powerful philosophy. *Mingei*, roughly translated into English as 'folk craft' or 'folk art', emerged in 20th-century Japan as a reaction against rapid modernisation. Propelled by prominent art theorist Sōetsu Yanagi and a group of potters, the movement valued the craftsmanship of ordinary, utilitarian objects made by nameless and unknown artists – like this garment. When Japanese farmers couldn't afford cotton, they turned thrifty, incorporating old futon bed coverings and other discarded fabric to create a patchworked sturdy, durable garment – an assembly work that provided a second life to ragged textiles. This emphasis on mending is at the core of Japanese craftsmanship, with evidence of repair often celebrated as a crucial part of the artwork itself. The person who assembled this coat to keep warm in the fields may not have aspired to create a piece of art, but works like this were the pillar of the Mingei Movement. Yanagi's ideas about beauty and frugality spread rapidly, and by the 1960s, consumer demand for folk crafts led to a 'mingei boom' – an ironic twist for the philosophy that was born out of resistance to mass production.

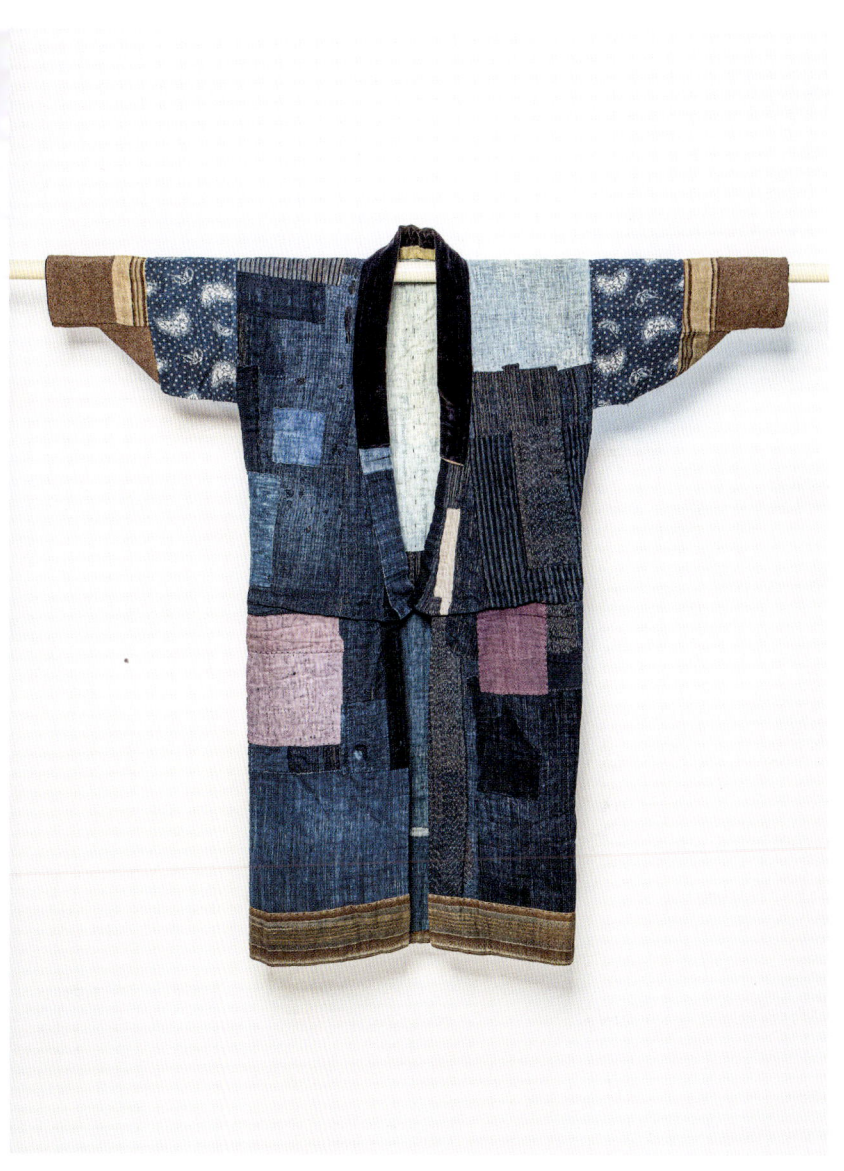

Farmer's Coat, 1920, cotton, indigo, 123 × 126 cm, Mingei International Museum, California

Whirligig with Woman Churning and Man Sawing, c. 1920

Quirky mechanised weathervane

Technically, a whirligig is any object that spins – or whirls – in the wind, and many have no practical use whatsoever. These amusing three-dimensional items are simply good fun. Whirligigs have been around since medieval times (even getting a mention in Shakespeare's *Twelfth Night*) but became ever more elaborate in late 19th-century America, evolving into sophisticated mechanisms displaying an individual artist's humour and taste. This one is both a whirligig and a weathervane. It shows daily activities of rural life: a man sawing wood and an apron-wearing woman churning butter under a dainty metal roof. When the wind blows, the weathervane activates, the wheel spins, the woman's arms move to pound the butter and the man's arms hurry to chop the log: a hive of industry. Whirligigs may have been crafted and sold to make extra cash in tough times (with amateur production increasing for this reason during the Great Depression). But life in rural America was demanding, and it's also possible that these quirky ornaments were just a diverting pastime.

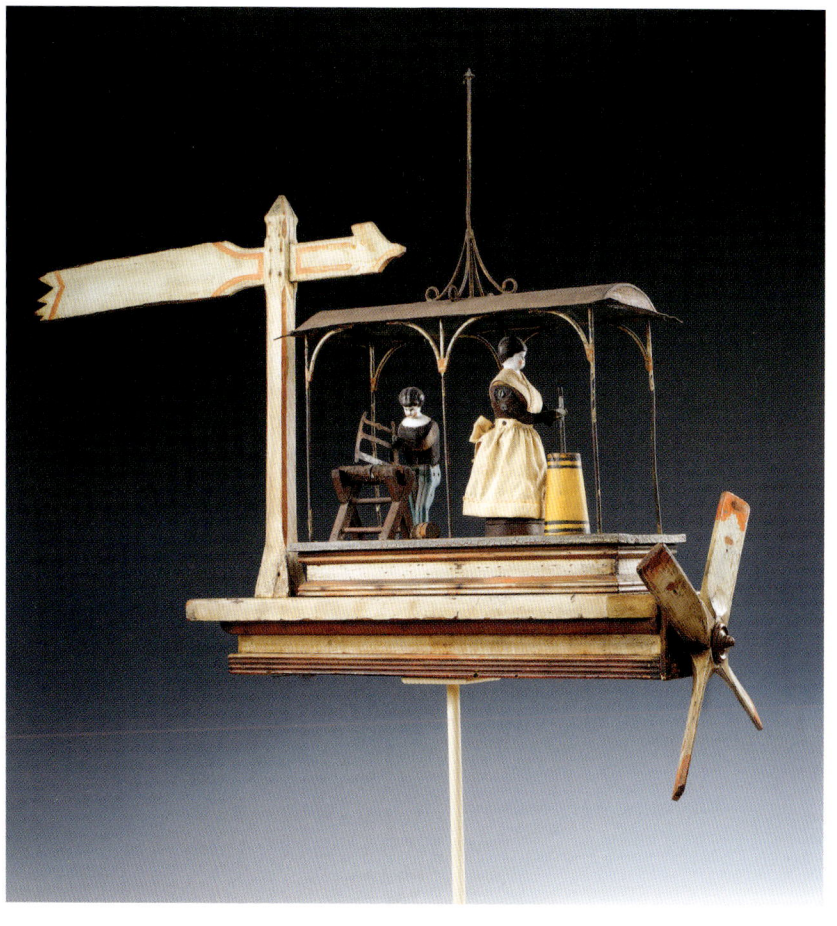

Whirligig with Woman Churning and Man Sawing, c. 1920, cut,
turned and painted wood; metal; cloth; porcelain doll parts, 72 × 83.8 × 32 cm, Smithsonian

Untitled (Yellow and Blue House with Figures and Dog), 1939

Storyteller of a Black nation

Bill Traylor was born into slavery, and spent most of his life after emancipation as a tenant farmer. After moving to Montgomery, Alabama, in his seventies, he found himself living on the streets, where he began to draw on discarded pieces of cardboard. This work is one of his earliest and represents many of the artist's familiar motifs, capped with an uncertain signature that betrays his lack of formal literacy. The house recalls the decades he spent working on the plantation; the dressed-up man, with his pointy, anvil-shaped shoes, personifies death; the ladder holds the promise of freedom; and the rifle and dogs symbolise systematic brutality against Black bodies. When Traylor's work was noticed and preserved by contemporaneous white artists, his style was lauded as 'primitive', but these simple silhouettes and shapes are a code, a unique language of symbols and storytelling. As a Black person in the segregated South, self-expression was dangerous; but here, in his own visual lexicon, Traylor offers a direct confrontation of violence, a vignette of America at a crossroads between slavery and civil rights.

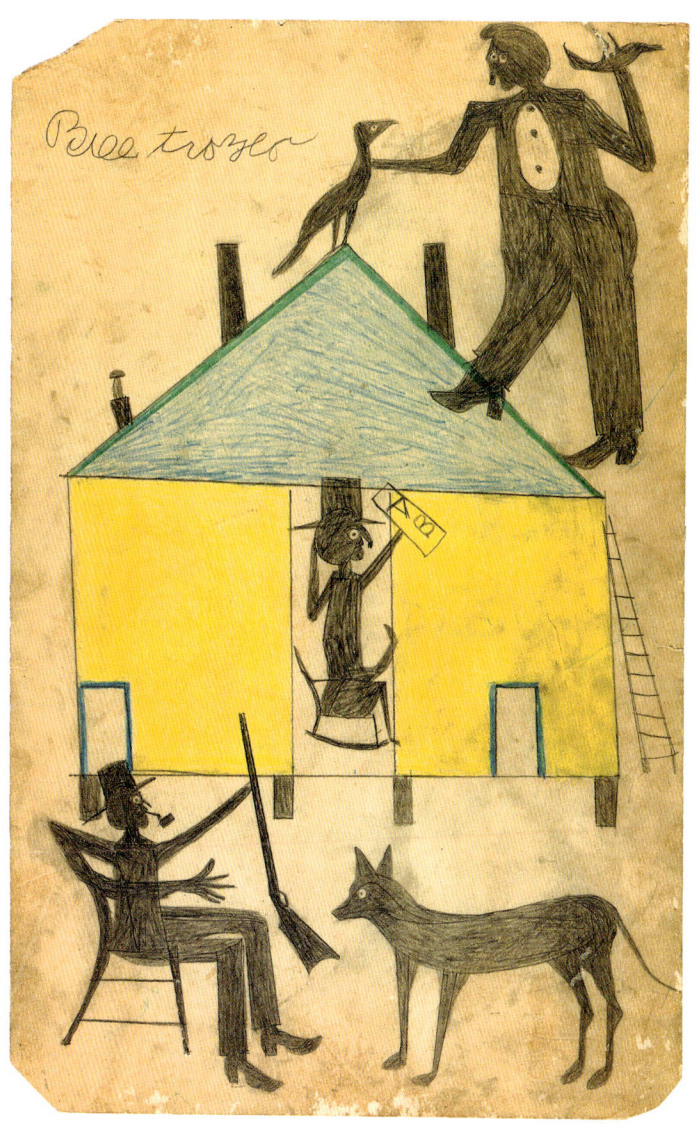

Bill Traylor, *Untitled (Yellow and Blue House with Figures and Dog)*, 1939, coloured pencil on cardboard, 56.5 × 36.2 cm, Smithsonian

WILLIAM H. JOHNSON

Street Life, Harlem, c. 1939–1940

Bold tribute to the Harlem Renaissance

This swaggy Black portrait chronicles a major culture-defining moment with verve and tenderness. American artist William H. Johnson had been living in Denmark and Norway with his Danish wife through the 1930s but returned to the States in 1938 to escape increasing Nazi sentiment in Europe. His use of bold colours, flattened representation and uneven proportions are all hallmarks of the Scandinavian folk art that inspired him. Night casts its blue and pink shadows onto the apartment buildings, and this poised couple is dressed to impress, perhaps on their way to one of Harlem's many jazz clubs – although their offhand glance tells us it's probably just another evening for them. Encapsulated in this paint-ing, the Harlem Renaissance was an incredibly fecund era of Black culture in America: an emergence and revival of music, literature and radical politics that coincided with the Great Migration of Black people fleeing the racist policies in the American South. Buoyed by this explosion of creativity, Johnson painted characters with the knack and expressive-ness of comic art. Together with intellectuals and artists such as Alain Locke, Langston Hughes and Duke Ellington, he pushed a bursting Harlem into the mainstream.

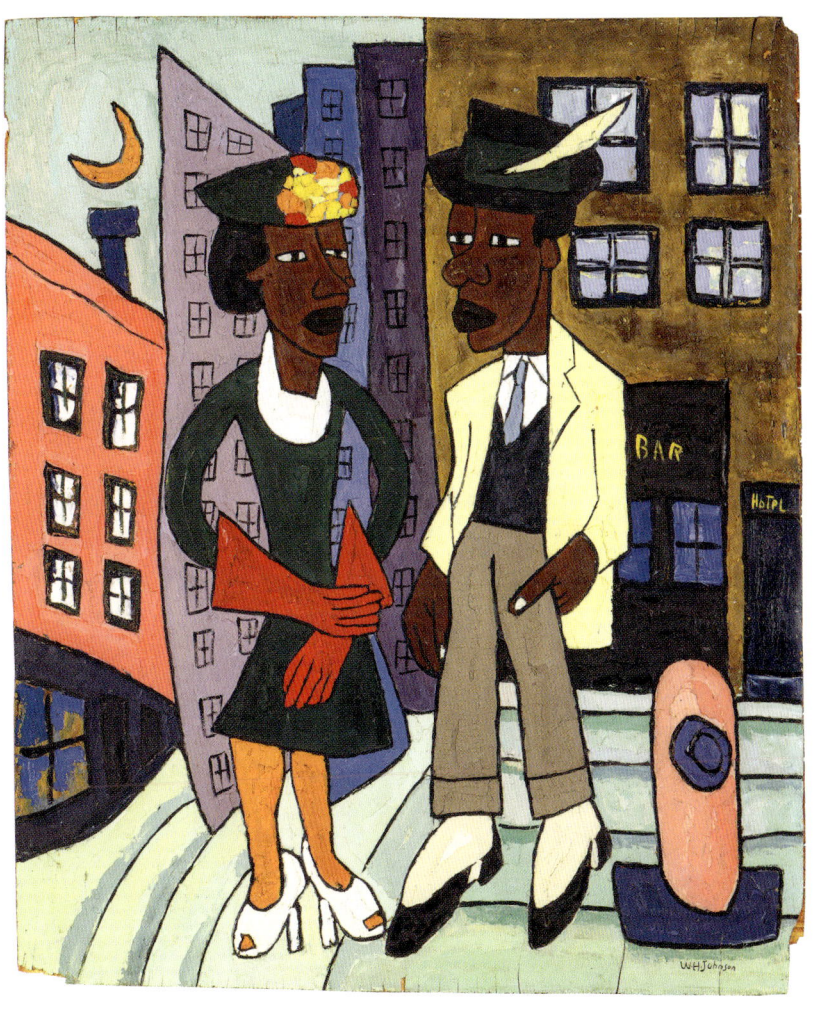

William H. Johnson, *Street Life, Harlem*, c. 1939–1940,
oil on plywood, 116 × 98 cm, Smithsonian

Catching the Thanksgiving Turkey, c. 1943

Nostalgic landscape from a folk art icon

It is an all-America landscape: a farm, a field, the first Thanksgiving snowfall and the anticipation of a turkey roast with all the trimmings. Anna Mary Robertson Moses, commonly known as 'Grandma Moses' for her numerous progeny (more than 30 great-grandchildren), began to paint aged 78 after severe arthritis caused her to stop embroidery. During the following three decades, she produced more than 1,500 works, frequently depicting hearty holiday rituals and other idealised American celebrations (like Ammi Phillips' repeated *Girl in a Red Dress* [p.54], she painted several versions of Thanksgiving scenes – still a relatively recent holiday in her time). No doubt this painting – which omits evidence of modern life such as telephone poles – struck a chord with a jaded wartime audience nostalgic for a bygone era. Moses' first paintings were sold for a meagre $3 and her first solo exhibition given the somewhat demeaning title, 'What a Farm Wife Painted', but by the 1950s she had acquired two honorary doctoral degrees and regularly broke attendance records with her shows.

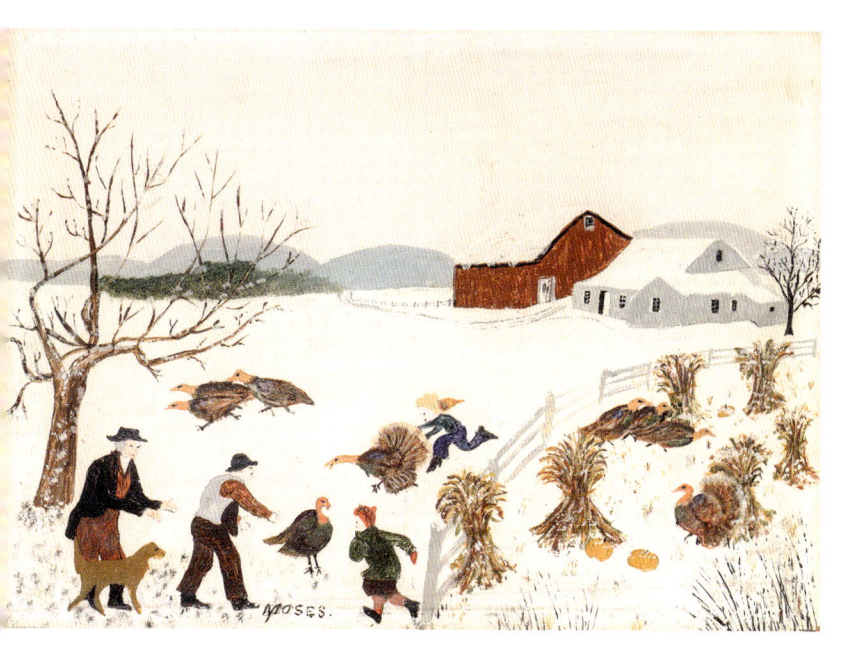

Grandma Moses, *Catching the Thanksgiving Turkey*, c. 1943,
oil on pressed wood, 30.5 × 40.6 cm, private collection

Subway Riders, 1950

Painting the daily grind

Ralph Fasanella's iconic painting of post-war New York City commuters is an ode to the good old subway as the centre of urban life. This is a picture of several individual journeys, but what drew him to the scene is that the people are not alone. '[The subway] pulls the city together, pulls people together in a magic way,' explained self-taught artist and union organiser Fasanella, who spent hours riding the network, sketching from life. The painting captures a period of affluence and social change in America's history. The 1950s was the golden age of capitalism, a major economic boom that meant more jobs and more money to spend – notice the line of colourful adverts above the passengers' heads promising bank loans, soap, coffee and cleaning products. But this was also the Civil Rights era, and in a multiracial metropolis like New York City, the subway was an equalising space. Here, people in suits and stiff hats sit alongside those in uniform, some carrying food shopping, others reading the sports section. 'They are about people and they should be seen by people,' Fasanella said of his paintings – and indeed, in 1995 this one became the first oil painting to be installed in an NYC subway station.

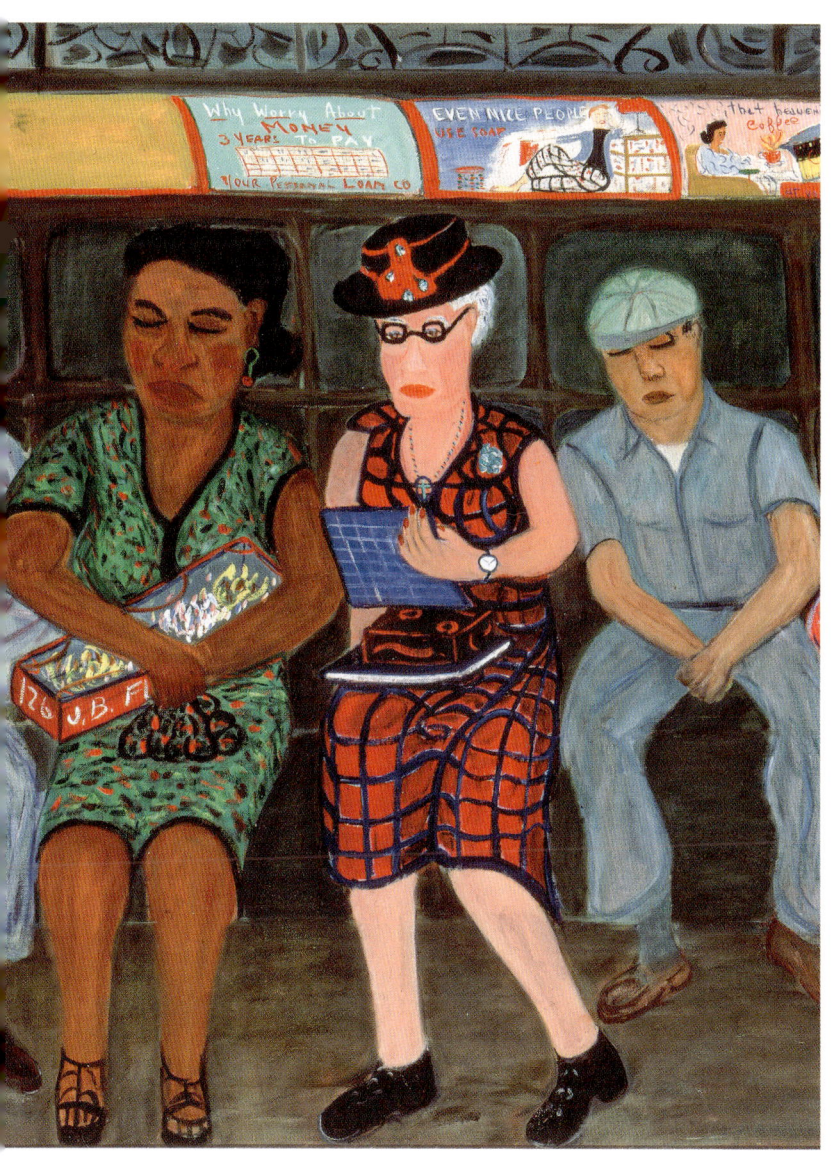

Ralph Fasanella, *Subway Riders* (detail; full work overleaf), 1950, oil on canvas,
152 × 71 cm, Fifth Avenue/53rd Street Station, New York City

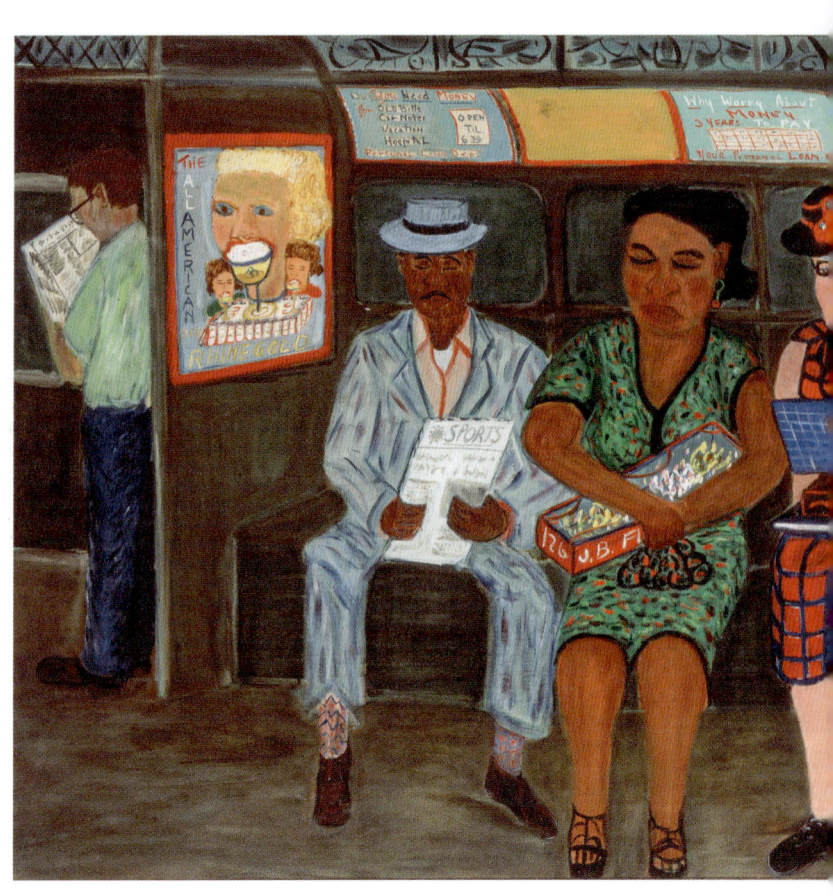

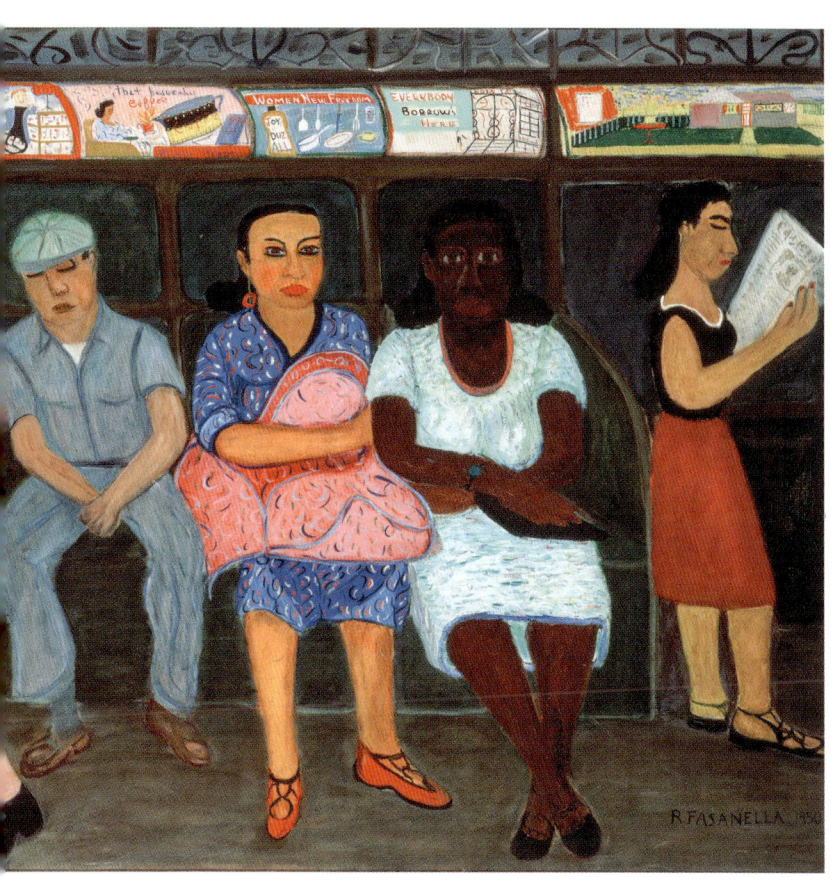

Picking Cotton, c. 1955

A colourful vision of backbreaking labour

Black women toil in the fields, filling bags with hand-picked cotton. Bent over and weighed down by their crop, the women are faceless, organised in two stacked rows that evade formal perspective. The bold colours and flat composition are characteristic of Clementine Hunter, who grew up in segregated Louisiana and worked on Melrose Plantation for most of her life. Entirely self-taught, Hunter painted scenes like this one from memory, making use of materials discarded by artists visiting Melrose Plantation Salon. She sold her first paintings for as little as 25 cents, but by the time she passed away aged 101, she had been exhibited in museums and sold for thousands of dollars, recognised as a significant insider chronicler of Black Southern plantation life. This painting is intensely uniform, the pretty pastel hues of the dusk sky and bright clothing at odds with the backbreaking work being carried out. Hunter's title is deliberately anonymous, reducing the women to their mechanical role. Who is picking the cotton? We don't know. This vibrant image may exude a naive, storybook-charm, but in it Hunter forces us to contemplate the labour performed by Black people in the American South.

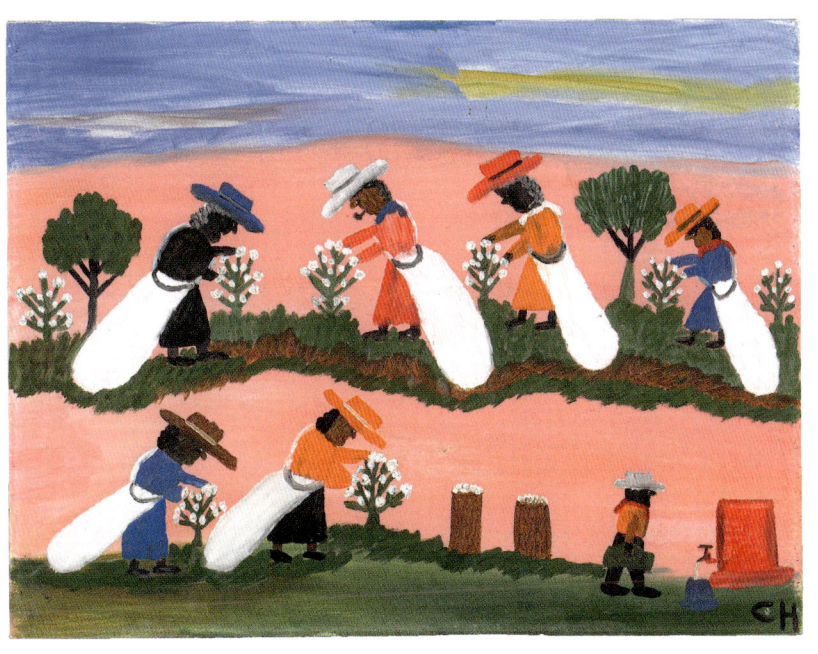

Clementine Hunter, *Picking Cotton*, c. 1955, oil on board,
50.8 × 61 cm, Minneapolis Institute of Art

Bug Kite, mid-20th century

Hand-painted toy

Kites are so popular in Japan that there's even a phrase for the obsession: *tako-kichi*, which means 'kite-crazy'. Japanese people have been tako-kichi since the 7th century, when kites were first introduced to the islands by Buddhist monks who flew them during religious and thanksgiving festivals. Kite-flying became a social activity during the Edo period, attracting a growing number of urban enthusiasts, especially from Tokyo. Kite-masters elevated simple constructions into prized collectibles via woodblock printing, traditional dyes and careful hand-painting. As interest soared, so did design: kites shaped like cranes, fish, dragons and turtles took to the sky, the animals symbolising longevity, prosperity and strength. This entrancingly sweet and modern bug kite recognises the cultural significance of insects in Japan as symbols of rebirth and seasons. But, of course, kites have evolved to become more than spiritual and symbolic objects: perhaps most importantly, they are toys, an exhilarating pastime for kite-crazy generations.

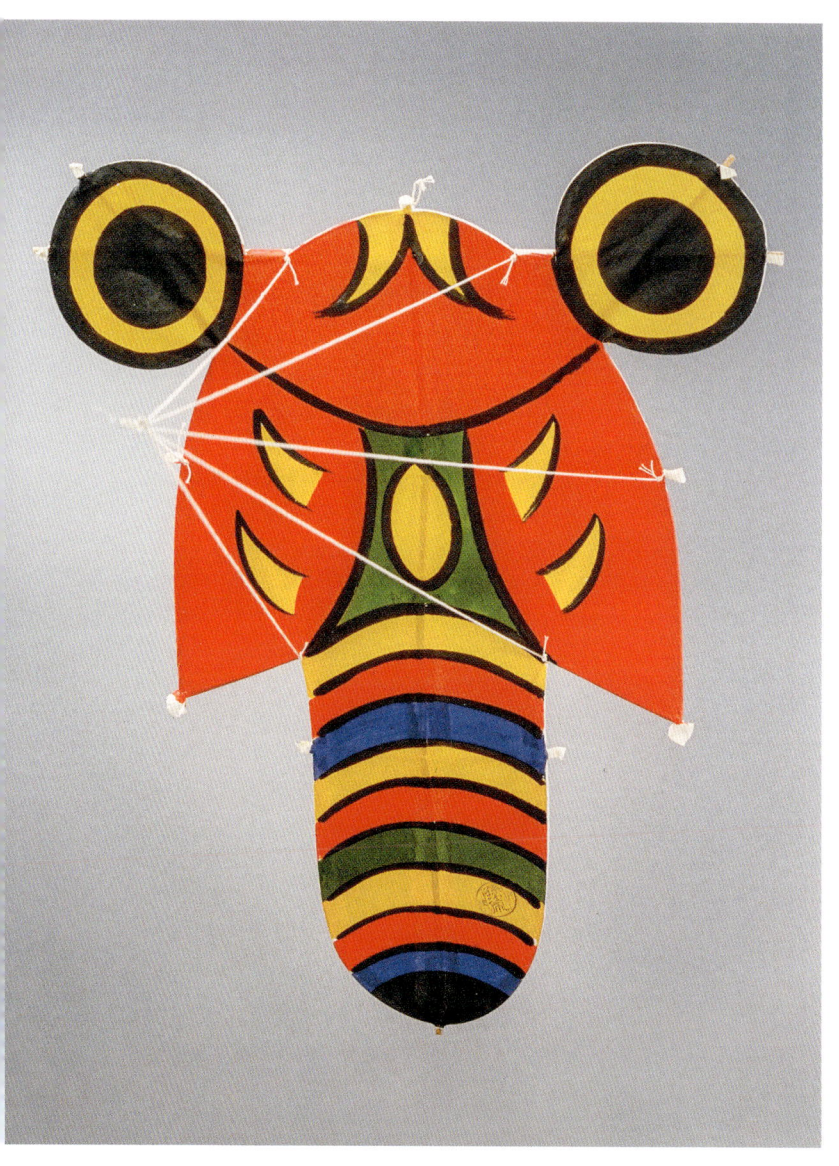

Bug Kite, mid-20th century, bamboo, paper, paint,
91.4 × 68.6 cm, Museum of International Folk Art

Dala Horse, mid-20th century

Iconic wooden animal

The legend goes that the first Dala horse was carved in 1716 from a scrap of wood by a Swedish soldier during the Great Northern War. He painted it with the only colour he had to hand: bright red iron oxide from the nearby mines. It's a charming but apocryphal story: references to wooden horses in Sweden's Dalarna province actually date back the 1600s. They were probably carved from the offcuts of furniture-making, and their decoration (typically featuring a whimsical bridle, harness and saddle) emulates a popular style of Scandinavian folk painting known as rose-painting, or *kurbits*. Also associated with Swedish furniture decoration, kurbits patterns include vivid gourds, swirls and flowers inspired by tales and mythology. Dala horses were originally toys for children, handmade during the long Scandinavian winters. Chances are, their creators never imagined that the stocky red horse would become a global sensation. But that's exactly what happened in 1939, when the Swedish pavilion at the New York World Fair erected a giant Dala horse statue. Mass production started, and the horse became more than a toy, but a national symbol and souvenir.

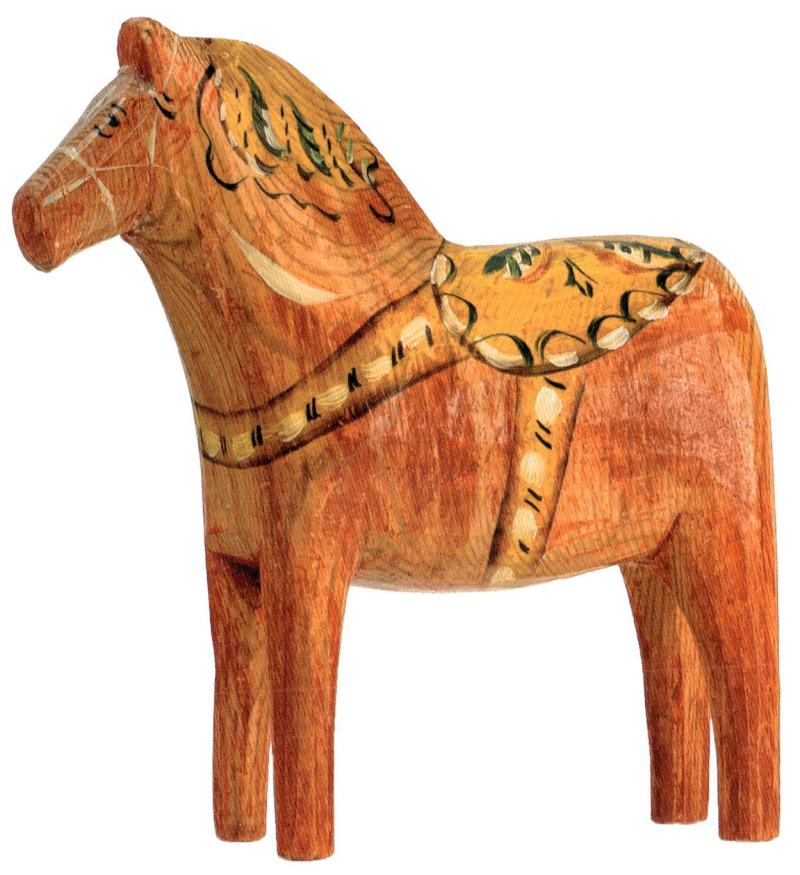

Dala Horse, mid-20th century, paint on carved wood

Matryoshka Dolls, mid-20th century

A peasant family

Despite being commonly known around the world as Russian nesting dolls, these wooden toys were not initially Russian. The nesting concept originated in China and travelled to Japan, eventually brought to Russia by Elizaveta Mamontova, who acquired a nesting doll as a souvenir on her travels in Asia. We don't know for certain whether Mamontova's Japanese model directly influenced doll maker Vasily Zvyozdochkin and painter Sergey Malyutin – who were both employed in the workshop of her art patron and entrepreneur husband – when they created the first set in 1892. Perhaps they were inspired by the Russian tradition of detachable Easter eggs. But it's easy to see why their early design was called *matryoshka*, or 'little matron': in their original set, a subdued peasant matriarch contains increasingly smaller doll family members, until you reach the tiny solid wooden baby at the centre. A popular toy since it was presented at the 1900 World Expo, matryoshka doll design evolved with cultural changes (initially becoming ever more ornate, and then simplified once again under Soviet rule). The understated appearance of these dolls, with their bare wood and inky outlines, suggests they date from the Soviet period.

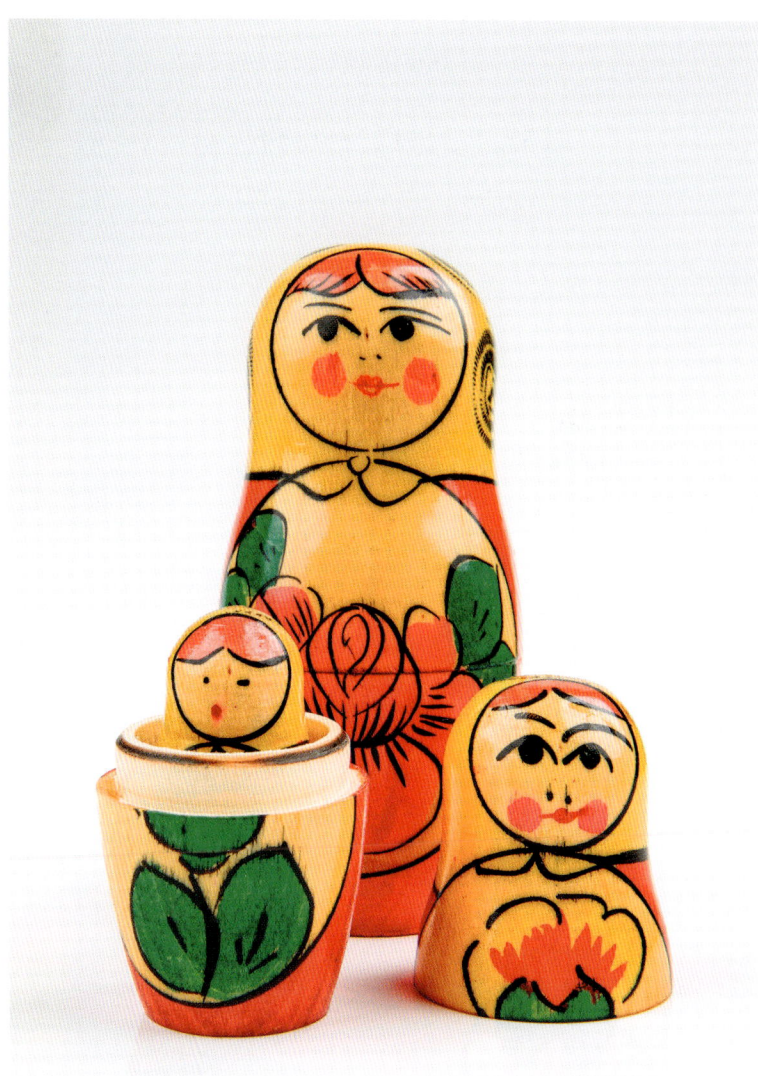

Matryoshka Dolls, mid-20th century, paint on carved wood

Bebado (Drunk), mid-20th century

Surreal, serial faces

A diffracted face seems to stretch like accordion bellows. The manifold eyes, ears, nose and mouth create a dizzying, surreal vision. There's little doubt about it, he's absolutely sloshed. And we can't help but feel as disoriented as he is. Antonio Roseno de Lima (known as ARL) was a nifty self-taught artist. He practiced woodturning and toy-making from a young age and photographed weddings to get by, until financial woes pushed him to live in a favela in São Paulo State, where he survived in modest conditions. He was also schizophrenic, a mental health condition that can cause delusions and disconnect from reality. That many of his portraits have several eyes could evoke his uncanny experience of the world – but also, perhaps, his enduring love of photography, the man's multiplied features reminiscent of photo negatives and double exposures. ARL was illiterate and so regularly asked friends to help him with the writing that often featured in his works, such as here where it says: 'I'm a very drunk, intelligent man. I was a man who never had love.' Whether this sad character is an expression of his own material and emotional struggles is unclear.

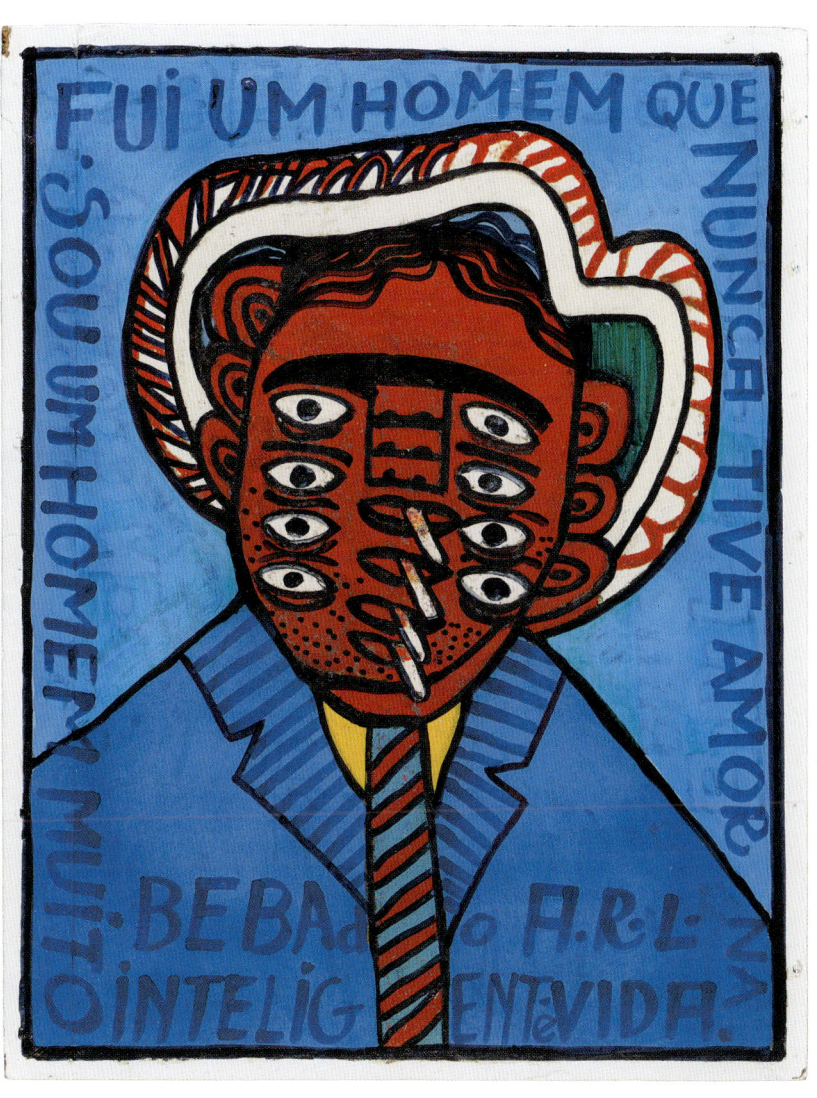

Antonio Roseno de Lima, *Bebado (Drunk)*, mid-20th century,
synthetic paint on cardboard, 58 × 46 cm, Collection de l'Art Brut Lausanne

Navajo Man, c. 1960

Relic from a medicine man

The dignified simplicity of this Navajo man exerts a cap-
tivating charm. Beyond his quiet appearance, he is both a
tribute to Native American culture and an embodiment of
extreme precarity. For Charlie Willeto, a Diné medicine man
and shepherd living on a New Mexico Navajo reservation,
this figurine was quite literally sustenance: Willeto sculpted
around 400 in his life and bartered these for groceries. He
worked with the humble materials he had to hand – pine
wood, house paint, natural dyes such as those his wife used
for weaving – and the result evokes a powerful Navajo rite.
Medicine men have performed important roles in Navajo
society as a living repository of ancestral practices and know-
ledge, including diagnosing illnesses, manipulating sacred
plants and leading ceremonies that connect with spiritual
realms. Among these traditional practices is a healing ritual
that involves the carving of human figurines displayed in
ceremonies, similar to Willeto's in size and style, and likely a
source of inspiration for his work. Sacred Navajo ritualistic
practices were traditionally kept secret from outsiders, and
so Willeto's work offers a rare – and controversial – glimpse
into the culture.

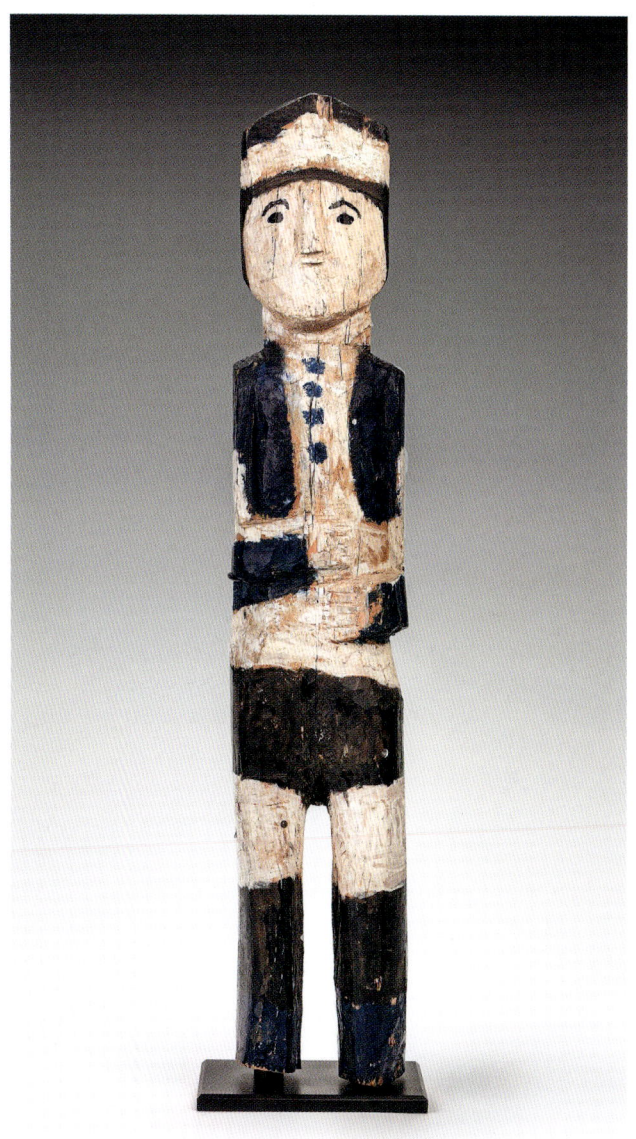

Charlie Willeto, *Navajo Man*, c. 1960, house paint on carved pine,
74.3 × 12.7 × 10.2 cm, Smithsonian

UNKNOWN ARTIST

Mola, c. 1960

Dressed to protest

Panama's indigenous Guna (or Kuna) women weavers can spend months producing an embroidered panel like this, designed for part of a blouse. Here, birds, dogs and sheep congregate towards Saint Francis, patron saint of animals. A mola is more than a hypnotically colourful garment: it's a form of enduring protest and resistance. Traditionally, Guna women painted their bodies with geometric designs using natural pigments, but this practice became more difficult after the Spanish colonisation. Conservative colonisers frowned upon body painting, pushing Guna women to find other canvases for these sacred stories. When cotton became available via 19th-century trade ships, Guna women invented the mola. Molas are works of spectacular – and patient – needlework compositions. Several layers of fabric are stacked together on a single panel, with motifs revealed through cutting layers of fabric and sewing down the patterns. In 1925, when the Panamanian government tried to impose a Westernised 'national' culture (banning Guna women from wearing traditional dress), the Guna people fought back, eventually declaring their independence. Today, mola designs remain potent symbols of Guna identity and sovereignty.

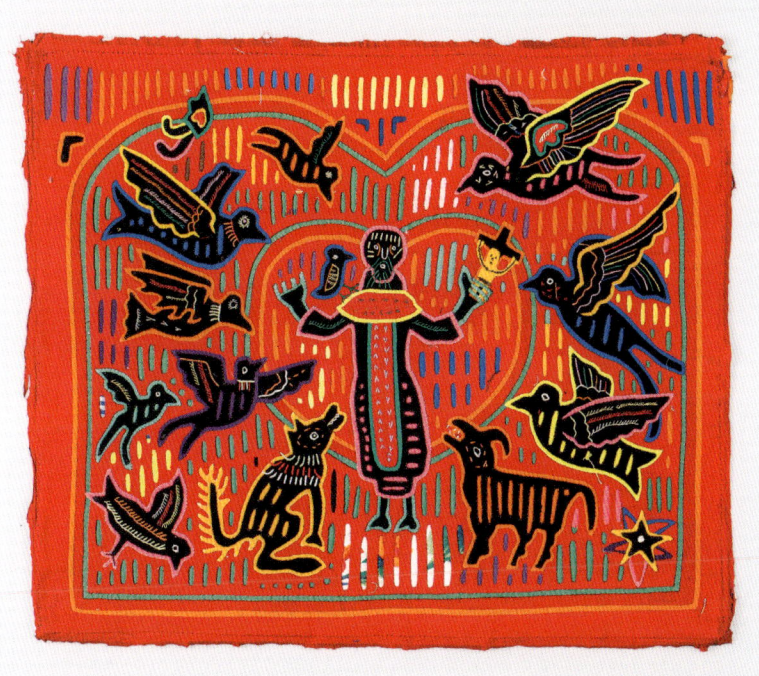

Mola, c. 1960, cotton, 39.5 × 48 cm, Museum of International Folk Art

Prayer Stone Wrapper, c. 1960

Precious wedding gift

This embroidered cotton handkerchief might recall a sampler at first, with the zigzagging frame and multiplicity of shapes and patterns. But this is a ceremonial cloth from Afghanistan, used by the persecuted Hazara Shi'a minority to wrap prayer stones during religious rituals. The hands depicted here are a nod to the 7th-century battle of Karbala, a significant historical event that saw two opposing Muslim factions fighting over competing claims to the Caliphate. The battle concluded with the martyring of Husayn, grandson of the Prophet Muhammad, and the sacrifice of his half-brother Abbas, who died after his hands were amputated during combat. Today, the namesake Al-Abbas shrine stands in Karbala in his honour, a major pilgrimage site for Shi'as around the world. The monument, as well as two hands depicted on this cloth, remind worshippers of Abbas's courage. Yet this hand-stitched homage was not intended to be shown in a museum; it's a domestic object, created by a Hazara woman as part of her dowry.

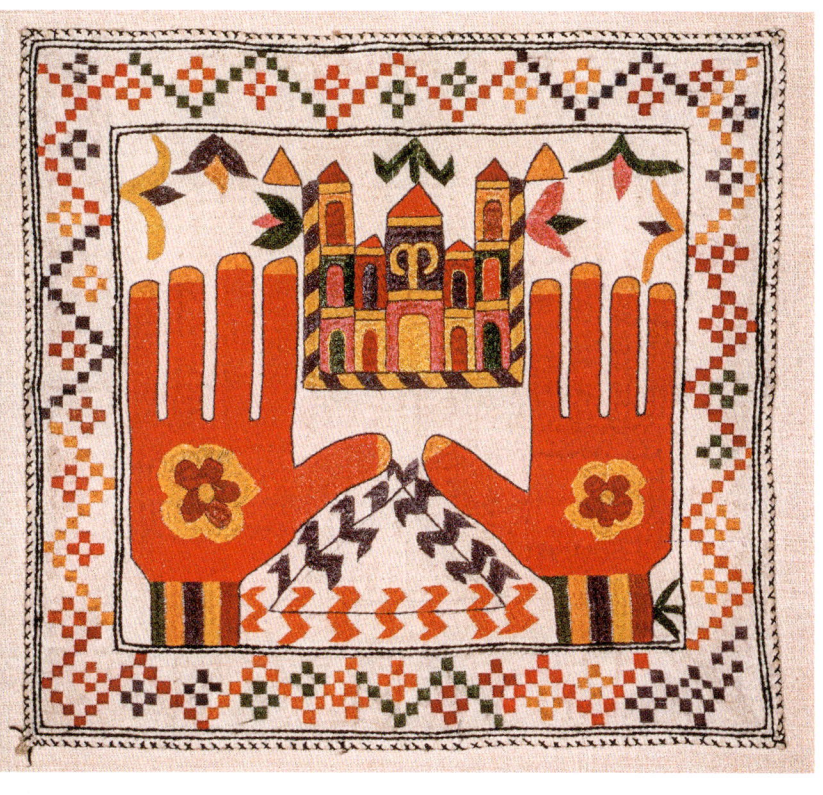

Prayer Stone Wrapper, c. 1960, cotton embroidery on a cotton ground,
30.5 × 34.3, Museum of International Folk Art

SAFIA FARHAT

The Bride, 1963

Weaving Tunisian women's rights

Here is an eye-catching bride who has it all: the resolve of a statue, the vibrancy of a painting, the luminosity of stained glass and the texture of a woven wall hanging. The woman's richly adorned clothes pay homage to Tunisia's mixed Arab, African and Amazigh (Berber) ancestry. This tapestry – assembled from various pieces of fabric – is a cross-cultural collage. The embroidered collar of the dress echoes that of a *jebba* robe, a traditional Tunisian garment, while the triangle patterns on the skirt evoke the Amazigh *fibula*: a piece of triangle-shaped jewellery widespread among North African tribes. Safia Farhat was a trailblazer, incorporating traditional crafts such as tapestry into modern Arab art. The first director of Tunisia's Institute of Fine Art post-independence in 1966, she also founded *Faïza*, the country's first feminist magazine. Through *Faïza*, Farhat bolstered public support for women's rights, helping to popularise progressive legislation in areas such as consent and divorce – a remarkable legacy in the Arab world to this day. Her mixed media works take Tunisian textile heritage as a starting point for developing a postcolonial visual identity – and one with women at its centre.

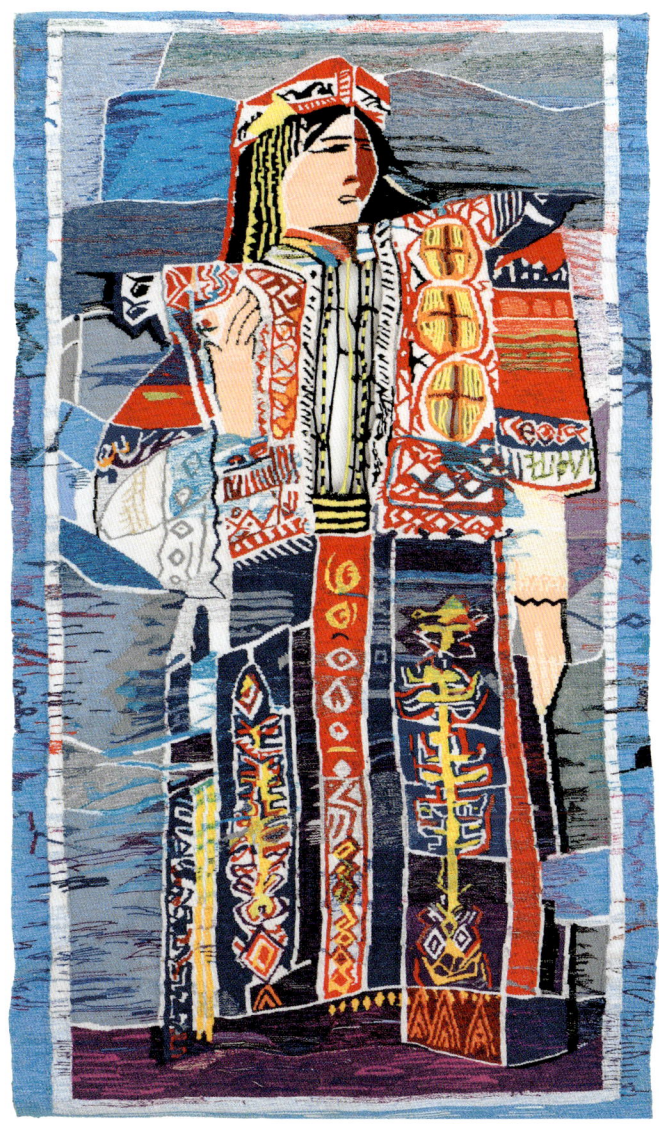

Safia Farhat, *The Bride*, 1963, tapestry, 172 × 100 cm, Barjeel Art Foundation

Les Deux Musiciennes (The Two Musicians), 1966

Radical vision of emancipation and happiness

Sometimes, a painting jumps out of the frame and sings. This is an Edenic garden, complete with elaborate plants, fountains and schools of fish. The artist, Baya Mahieddine (known simply as Baya), could only dream of such comforts and pleasure when she was a young, orphaned *indigène* (colonial subject) during the French rule of Algeria. Baya was adopted by a French intellectual who brought her self-taught talent to the notice of art dealers, arranging for an exhibition of her work in Paris, 1947, when Baya was just 16. The show drew accolades from the likes of Picasso and surrealist André Breton, the latter gushing that she would be 'the rocket that launches the new age'. He was right. After Algeria gained independence in 1962, Baya was at the forefront of the Aouchem art movement, which recognised the importance of folk art and Indigenous symbols as part of a liberated Algerian identity. Her work has been variously described as naive, surrealist, primitive and modern, but Baya resisted these Western categorisations. Her oeuvre is characterised by recurring motifs: (only ever) women, vegetation, animals and musical instruments, rendered in vibrant colours. It's a defiantly joyful world – at odds with the uneasy childhood and political violence she endured.

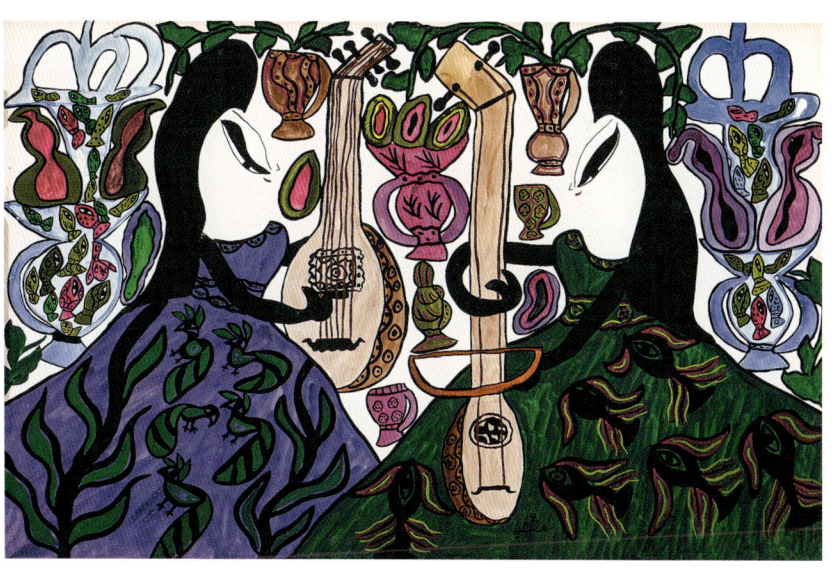

Baya, *Les Deux Musiciennes*, 1966, gouache and graphite on paper,
98 × 148.5 cm, Mathaf, Arab Museum of Modern Art, Qatar

War is a Terrible Beast, 1968

Farm animals dazed by war's unsatiated appetites

A hungry beast with rotten teeth digests stupefied animals: a horse, rooster, pig, cows and more. Trapped in the belly of this green monster, the farm animals eye us as witnesses to a horror scene. Beneath this painting's childlike motifs is a serious matter: war. The presence of livestock familiar to Ukrainian village life creates a striking visual dissonance. The hapless animals are not where they should be, and war – represented in this terrible, ugly, grotesque creature – exhibits its devastating power. Maria Prymachenko, one of Ukraine's most beloved artists, became a self-taught painter after learning embroidery at a young age. There is indeed something stitch-like about the layered composition in this painting and the texture of the beast's body. Prymachenko painted this during the Cold War, when tensions between nuclear superpowers nearly pushed the world off a precipice – but such geopolitical strife is not a thing of the past. Russia marched into Ukraine in February 2022, causing hundreds of thousands of casualties and the biggest refugee crisis in Europe since World War II. The beast can change faces, yet its horrors remain the same.

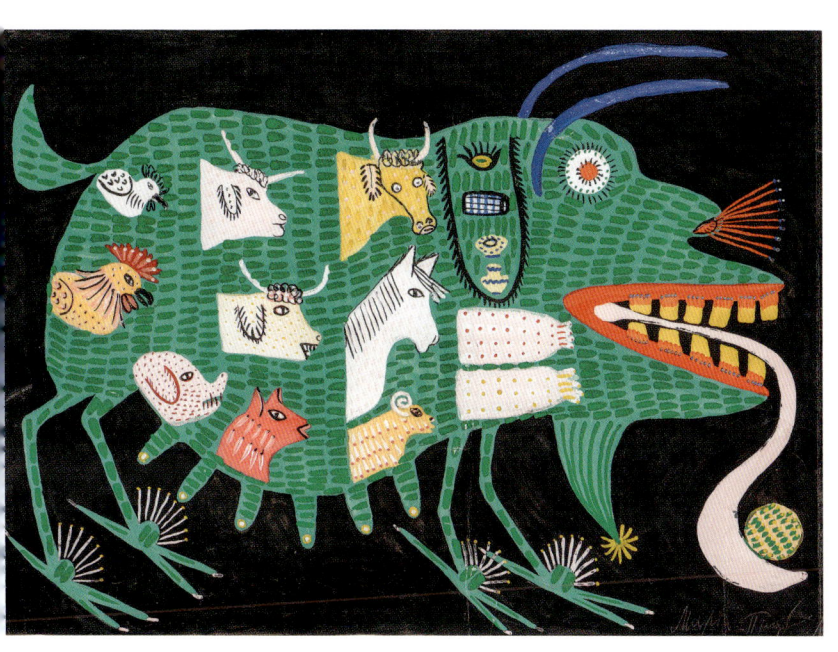

Maria Prymachenko, *War is a Terrible Beast*, 1968, gouache on paper, private collection

Haitian Landscape, 1973

An imagined paradise

It's a dreamy vignette of labour and plenty, but behind this veneer are the hardships experienced by Haitians under the dictatorial rule of the Duvalier dynasty (1957–1986), which pushed rising numbers of 'boat people' to American shores. Self-taught artist Joseph Jean-Gilles was born in Haiti but spent most of his adult life abroad. This lush, Edenic landscape is a reclamation: an expression of nostalgia and love for his homeland. Eschewing the traditions of Haitian folk painting – which tend to focus on historical scenes and Voodoo symbolism – Jean-Gilles' work seems to exist outside time. Here, orderly agrarian scenes are rendered with careful precision, far from the poverty, disease and natural disasters that have ravaged the country and thrown the lives of Haitian people into chaos. There are echoes of Henri Rousseau's (p.74) flattened and brightened jungles, and indeed both painters share a fantastical style – a perspective that allows them to imagine a new world.

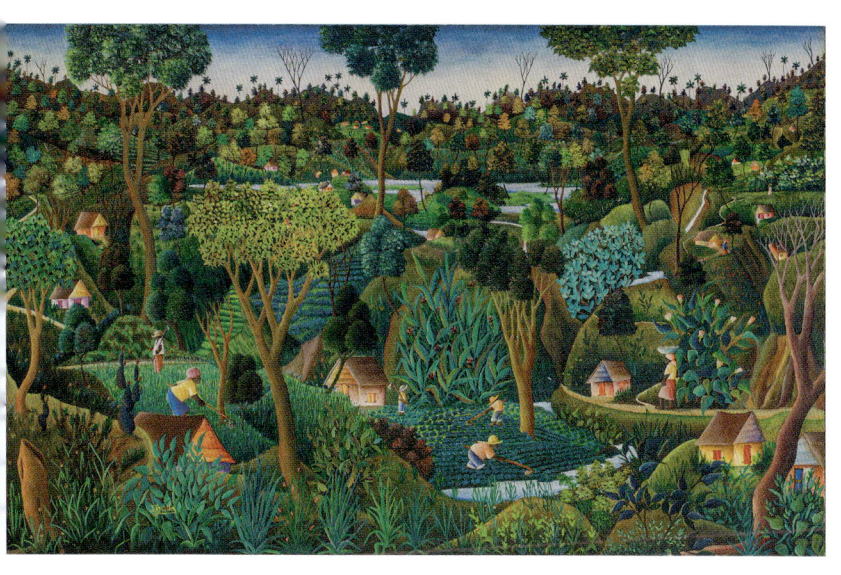

Joseph Jean-Gilles, *Haitian Landscape*, 1973, oil on canvas,
76.2 × 122 cm, Art Museum of the Americas

Basket, c. 1978

Personified storage solution

This is both a basket and a sculpture. Someone has gone to great lengths to craft its womanly shape, down to the dangling tasselled earrings. Basketry is an ancient craft in India, one mainly performed by women and often communally. Baskets were produced for multiple purposes: not just a place to store household goods, but also used in religious rituals (used to carry offerings such as sweets). No basket is truly the same, though. Their appearance and style vary with the availability of different materials, from palm leaves, cane and twigs to grass obtained after the monsoon. This one was made from reeds, like many ancient baskets, and produced in the East Indian state of Bihar. Information about its origin is sparse, but the region is known for creating human form basketry representing old tales, myths and legends taken from epic poetry. Some traditions see basket forms of Lord Krishna and his consort Radha replay their divine love story; one can imagine the awe and excitement at seeing the baskets come to 'life' in these community gatherings.

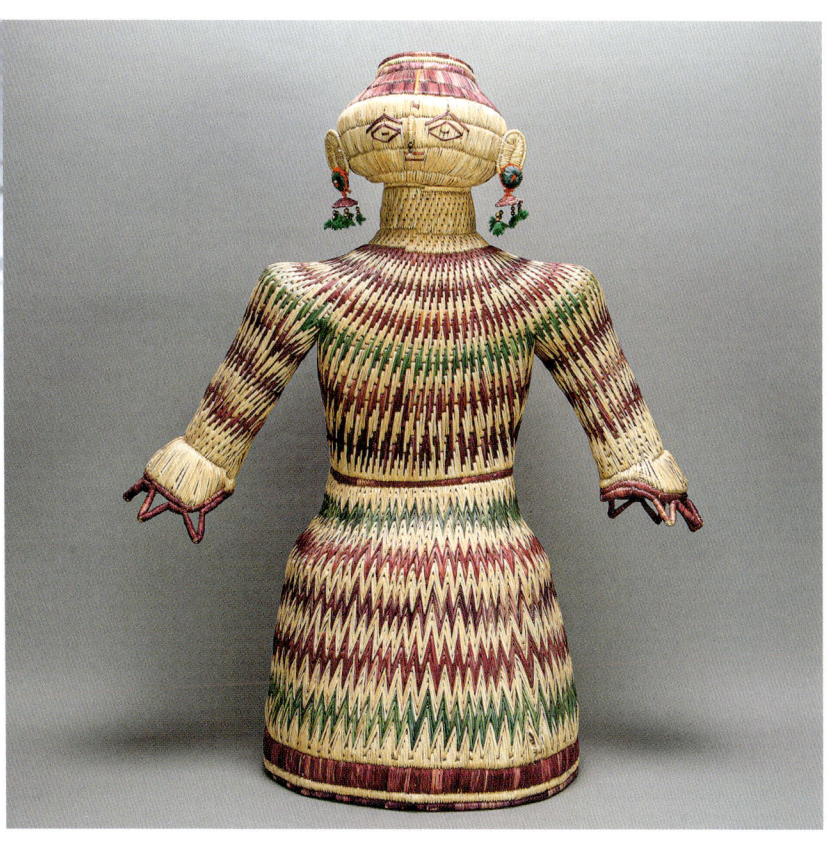

Basket in the Shape of a Woman, c. 1978, reeds, pigment,
76.2 × 71 cm, Museum of International Folk Art

AIDS Memorial Quilt, 1985–

A powerful expression of collective grief

This is the largest piece of community folk art in the world: a quilt commemorating the lives lost to HIV/AIDS, in which over 50,000 panels – each approximately the dimensions of a grave – memorialise more than 110,000 people. The project began in the 1980s, when Cleve Jones and other LGBTQ+ activists wrote the names of their friends lost to the illness on placards and taped these to the San Francisco Federal Building. The signs looked like an enormous patchwork quilt, and Jones was inspired. At the time, the social stigma of the illness meant that many of those who died from AIDS-related causes passed away without funeral services. The communal tapestry provided an opportunity for survivors to remember and celebrate the lives of their loved ones. The quilt toured the States through the 1980s, and as publicity increased, so did submissions: family members who didn't feel able to mourn openly stitched panels and posted them across the country. 'We tapped into a nationwide sense of grief,' said Mike Smith, one of the project's co-founders. Now weighing more than 50 tonnes, the quilt is the work of thousands of people – members of the LGBTQ+ community and allies, activists and suburban mothers. It is still being added to today.

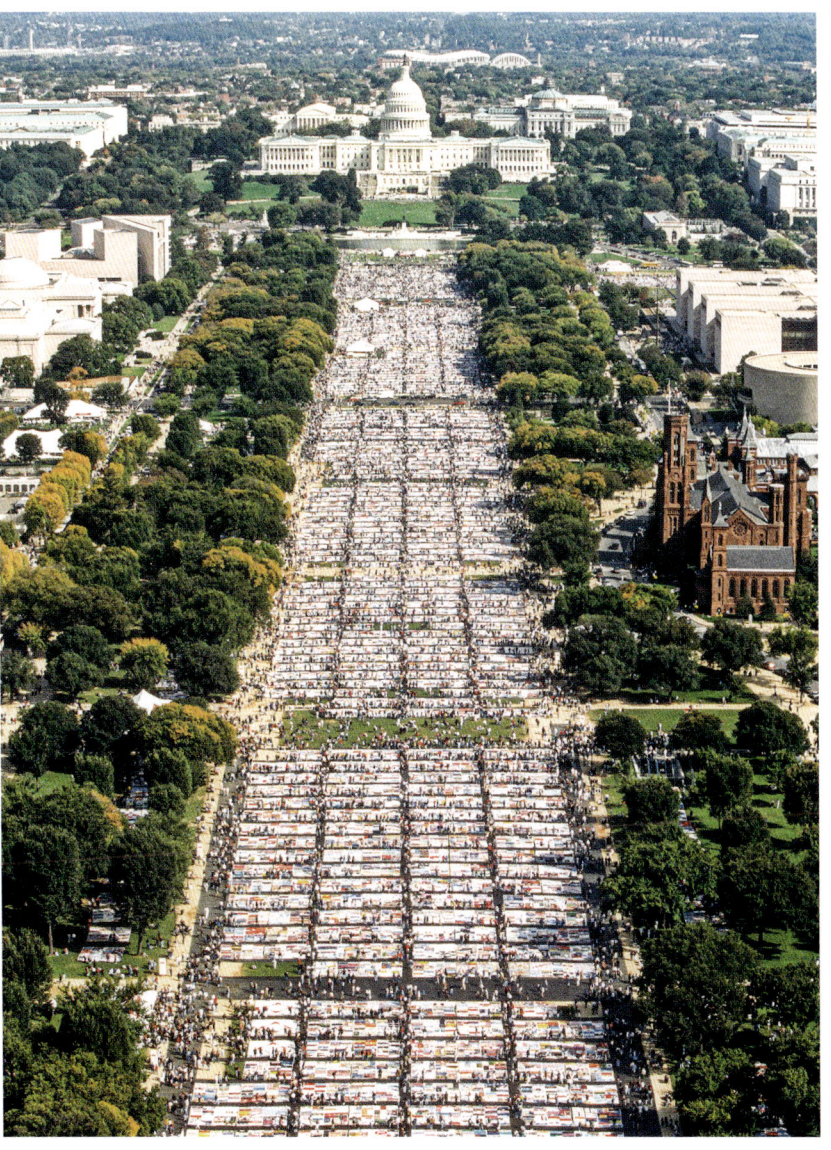

AIDS Memorial Quilt, 1985 onwards, various materials, over 120,000 m². Above: the quilt displayed in Washington, D.C., 1996. Overleaf: individual panels from the quilt.

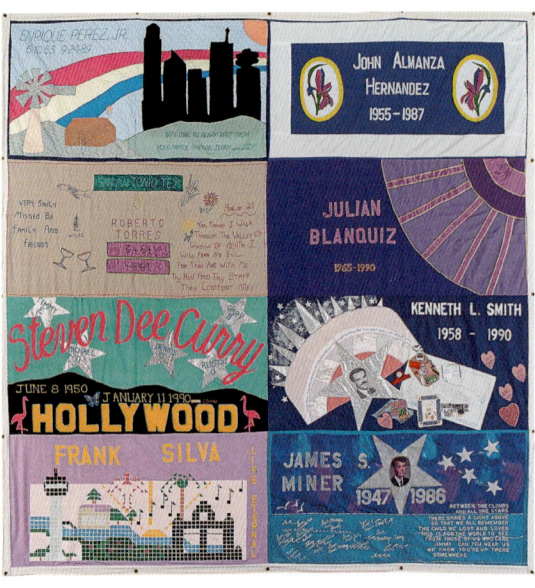

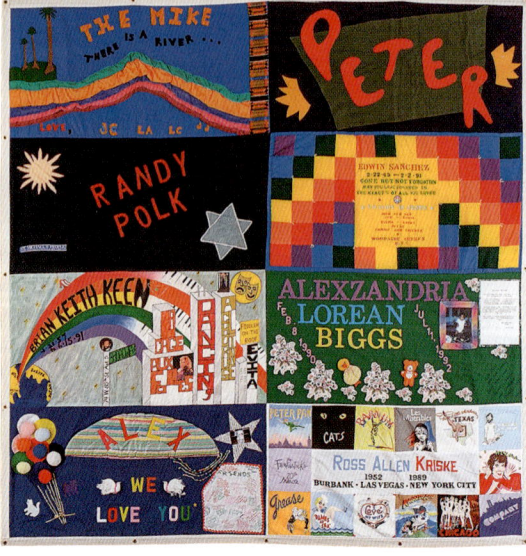

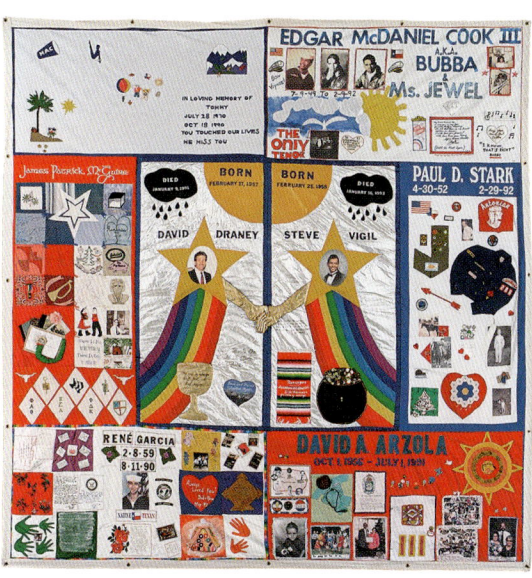

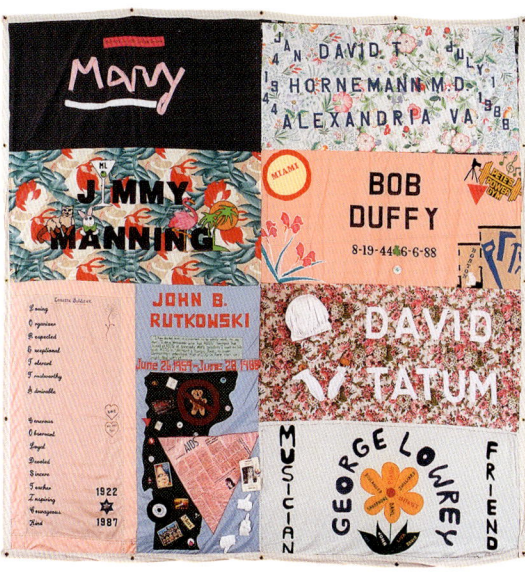

Alebrije (Pink Dragon), c. 1985

Fantastical beast

Zoomorphic fantastical creatures appeared to Pedro Linares during a fever-induced vision in 1936 when he was 30 years old. He dedicated the rest of his life towards bringing them into being as vibrant, papier-mâché figures which he called *alebrijes*, catapulting him into the canon of Mexican folk art. Linares borrowed from the existing practice of *cartonería*, playful devotional sculptures traditionally featured in Mexican religious celebrations – but his hybrid animals were unlike those seen during festivities. With its psychedelic colours and reptilian allure, this winged dragon symbolises the traditional spiritual guides who help souls cross to other realms in Mexican culture. From winged donkeys to roosters with bull horns, aquatic beasts to eagle-headed lions, Linares' magnetic icons caught the attention of contemporaries Diego Rivera and Frida Kahlo. His work has not only influenced Mexican folk art through countless renditions, but also popular culture – the 2017 Pixar film *Coco* included winged alebrijes. Since 2007, Mexico City has hosted a yearly alebrijes parade, and Linares' descendants continue fulfilling new orders to this day.

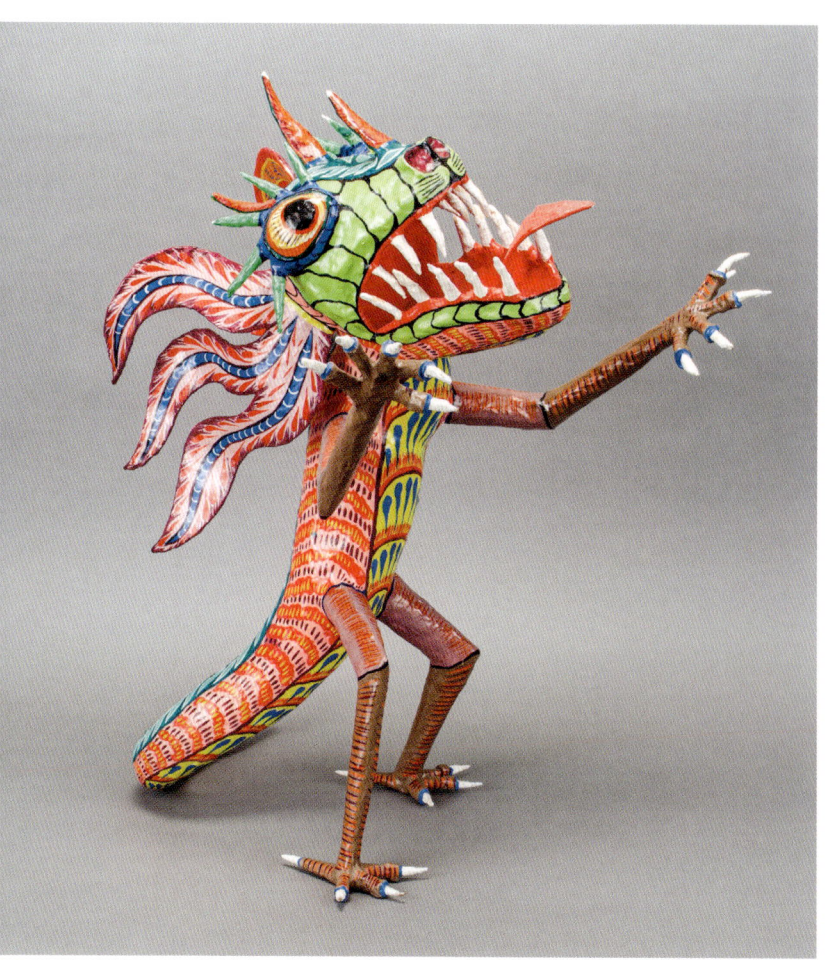

Pedro Linares, *Alebrije* (*Pink Dragon*), c. 1985, papier-mâché, paint,
56 × 38 × 52 cm, Museum of International Folk Art

Salvation Mountain, 1989

Candy-coloured altar of universal love

This public sculpture in the Californian desert was divinely whispered to its artist, local resident Leonard Knight, who believed God wanted him to build a mountain. In fact, he built two – the first site collapsed under heavy rains five years after construction began, but undeterred, Knight re-assembled the site with 'more smarts' the second time round to ensure it lasted. Made from tyres, scrap metal, clay and straw, and covered with half a million gallons of latex paint, the scale of this man-made mountain vastly exceeds this page: between four and five stories high and nearly 50 metres wide. Designated as a folk art site in 2000 by the Folk Art Society of America, the giant installation is both a toxic nightmare and a powerful altar of universal love, repentance and Gospel. It even features chapels where weddings can be officiated. Knight lived onsite in a fire truck for almost 30 years, giving free tours until his health deteriorated. People visiting the site over the past three decades have donated paint and worked for its upkeep, touched by the eccentricity of the place and the resolve of its outlandish creator.

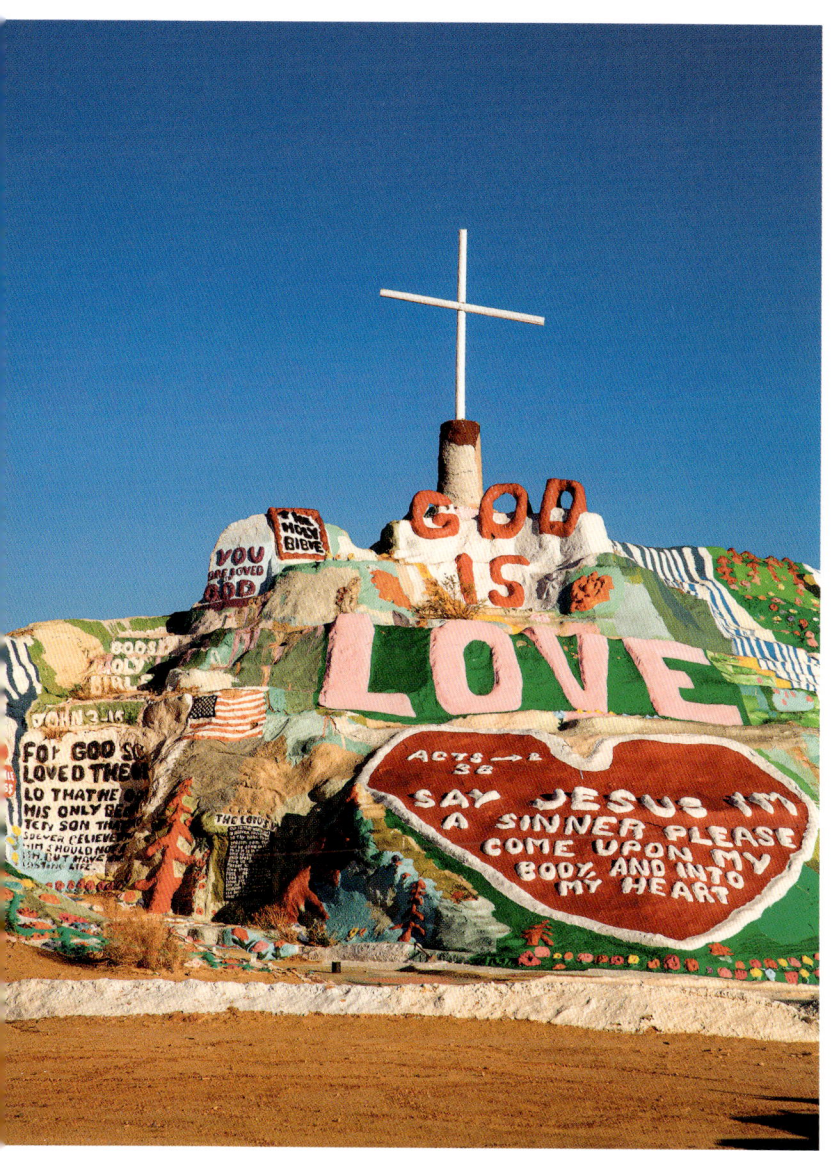

Leonard Knight, *Salvation Mountain*, 1989, adobe bricks,
car tyres, latex paint, 15 × 46 m, Niland, California

Cane with Man and Pistol, 1991

A charmingly unconventional accessory

We don't tend to think of canes as art, and yet this walking stick – made by small-town Kentucky-native Denzil Goodpaster – is nothing short of a sculpture. Two years after retiring from a life spent farming tobacco on his family's plot, his neighbour showed him a cane carved into a snake. Goodpaster's interest was piqued. Confident he could do better, he set to work with a humble pocketknife and leftover wood. His fabulously strange creations morphed into a distinctive style. The man – so elongated he appears to have been stretched – and comparatively diminutive pistol on this cane are typical Americana lore (Goodpaster also carved canes into cowboys, bikini-clad cheerleaders and even Dolly Parton). The painting here is sealed under plastic resin, adding protection and shine: it's meant to be admired. Goodpaster's work recalls 19th-century American cane art, popular when gentlemen 'wore' canes as status symbols and fashion accessories rather using them as than walking aids. Goodpaster's canes became so recognisable that other local folk artists imitated him, and in the 1980s he received institutional fellowships in recognition of his work and influence.

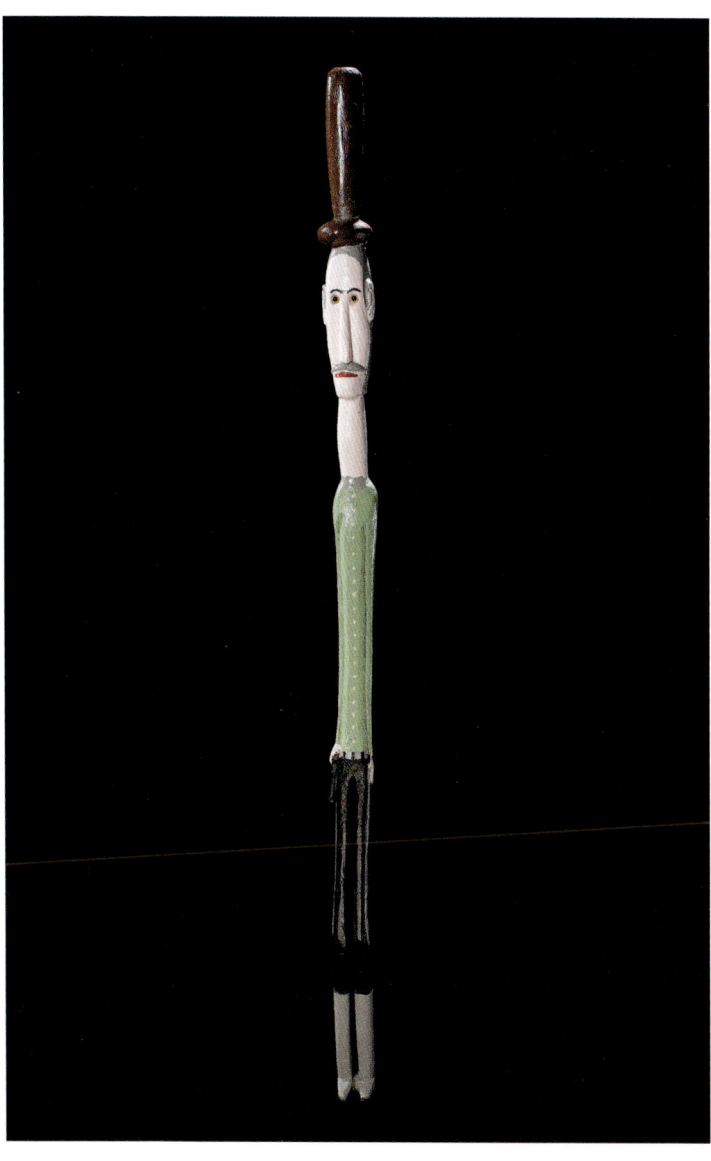

Denzil Goodpaster, *Cane with Man and Pistol*, 1991,
carved and painted wood and plastic resin, 101.9 × 6 × 5.6 cm, Smithsonian

OTESIA HARPER

Coke Covers the World, 1992

The American liberal dream

Mississippi-born seamstress Otesia Harper has been making quilts for more than 80 years, learning the craft from her grandmother. This quilt's visual geometry recalls the traditional grid pattern her American South forebears adopted, but there's a twist. Unlike the biblical motifs of Harriet Powers' creations (p.64), Harper's punchy designs feature overt reflections on contemporary culture and politics. Here, she pairs a patriotic palette with wry commentary on American imperialism and consumerism. Like Andy Warhol's proliferating Campbell's soup cans, Harper mimics the uniformity and repetition of advertising, each hand-stitched panel offering the same product. 'Coke covers the world,' it says, in charmingly wobbly stitch – a clever double entendre. Is this cover warming and protective, or concealing? In Harper's quilt, the entire world is an island floating in a Coke-dominated sea, speaking to the American cultural supremacy of the 1990s. The Soviet Union had collapsed and Western liberalism rushed to fill the void: floods of Coca Cola, conquering the world to the beat of Nirvana, Madonna and Michael Jackson.

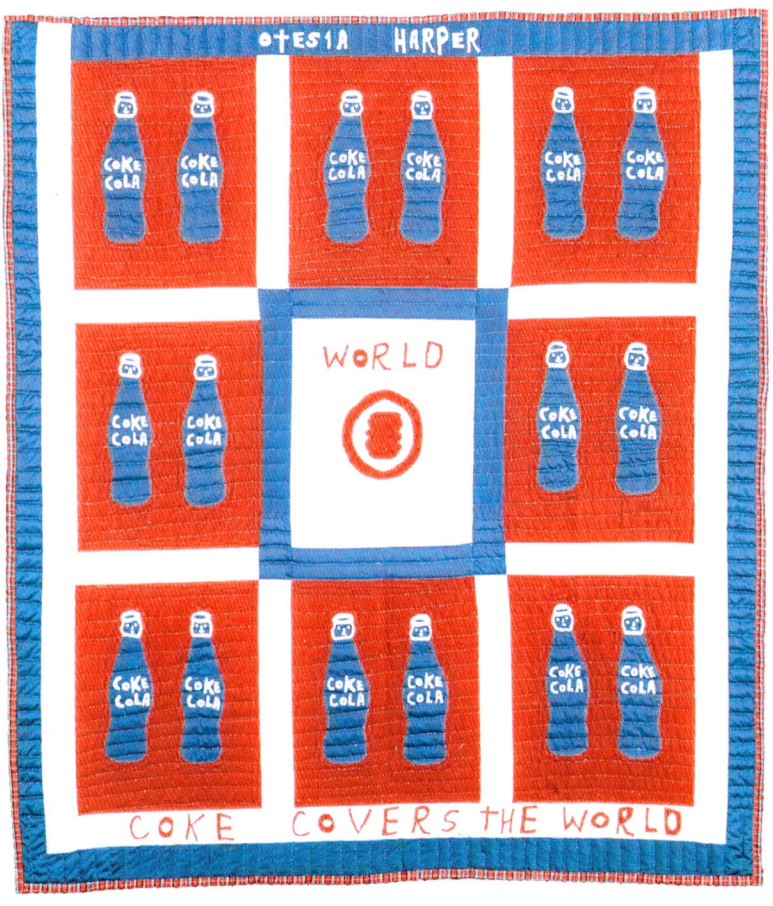

Otesia Harper, *Coke Covers the World*, 1992, appliquéd and stitched fabric,
205.7 × 188.6 cm, Smithsonian

Anwerlarr Angerr (Big Yam), 1996

Ancestral swirls

The Dreaming is an Aboriginal mythical time and place that has a beginning but no definite end, like the innumerable, sinuous lines of this painting. For Indigenous Australians, the Dreaming (also called 'Everywhen') encompasses a time when the land was inhabited by ancestral figures, an important mythology that helps affirm how they see themselves in the world. Western translations of the concept are vague; indeed, anthropologist William Stanner said it was best understood by non-Aboriginal people as 'a complex of meanings'. Perhaps this is what we're looking at. Renowned artist Emily Kame Kngwarreye's painting is several things at once: undulating lines look like the root system of yam in cherished soil, the steps of an anonymous pacer, the ruminations of a fecund mind, knotty filaments and fibres. During the 1980s, Kngwarreye was part of a collective of women artists in the remote desert area known as Utopia, who initially made batik inspired by traditional body- and sand-painting patterns, later translating these fine lines onto canvas. Like many folk artists, Kngwarreye grew up in a humble home and had a late but prolific artistic journey, producing more than 3,000 paintings – many depicting the Dreaming – in an eight-year career.

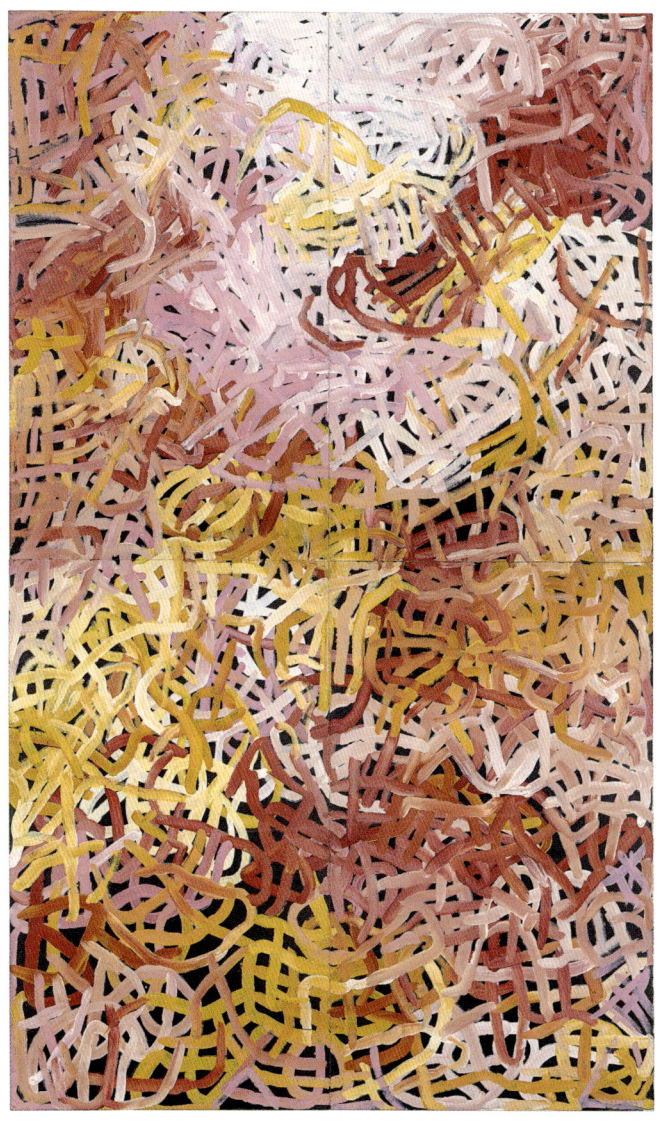

Emily Kame Kngwarreye, *Anwerlarr Angerr* (*Big Yam*), 1996, synthetic polymer paint on canvas, 401 × 245 cm, National Gallery of Victoria, Melbourne

Untitled (Harvest), late 20th–early 21st century

From dust to canvas

Jivya Soma Mashe is perhaps singlehandedly responsible for reviving the ancient tribal art form of Warli painting. Traditionally practised on special occasions by groups of married women, Warli art was painted on the red-toned walls of mud houses. The women used rice flour to create a stark white paste and worked with the chewed end of a bamboo stick, creating high-contrast images depicting fertility rites and weddings. Mashe's story is an unusual one. The artist started drawing in the dust aged just seven after losing his mother, adopting the visual schema of the art he had observed Warli women painting. Later in life, Mashe was the first Warli artist to paint on canvas and paper, modernising the ancestral practice and granting it a newfound permanence. Freed from the constraints of working on rough mud walls, his work is more a delicate expression of the form, filled with extraordinary detail and dynamism. This painting recalls the communal heritage of Warli art: a harvest that brings villagers, cattle, vegetation, mountain and sun together in a harmonious scene.

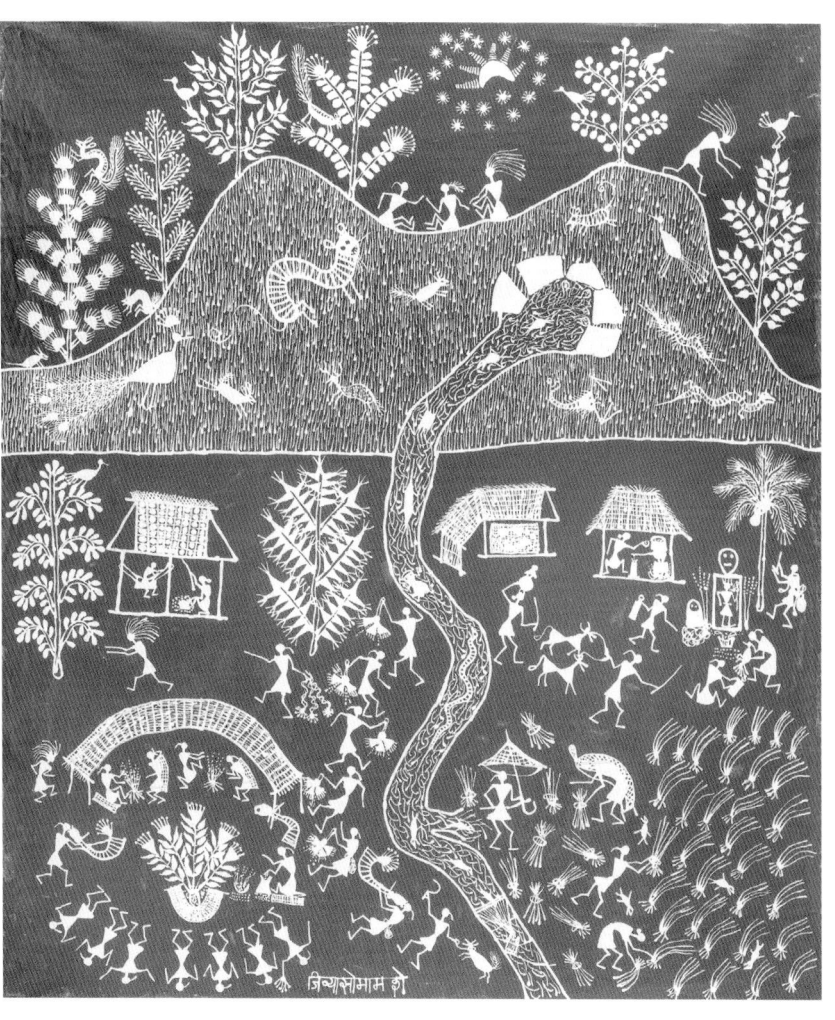

Jivya Soma Mashe, *Untitled* (*Harvest*), late 20th–early 21st century,
natural pigments on cloth, 94.5 × 82.5 cm, Museum of Art and Photography, Bengaluru

OSCAR SOTENO

Tree of Life, c. 2006

Colourful family tree

Oscar is not the first Soteno to play with clay. Born into a Metepec family of artisans in Mexico, he is the third generation in a lineage of respected traditional potters and ceramicists. The Sotenos, who still maintain inter-generational workshops, were deeply influenced by the boom in Mexican folk art during the 1930s and 1940s, which saw a renewed interest in craftsmanship and Indigenous art following the Mexican Revolution. 'Trees of life' are a Mexican folk art tradition going back centuries: painted ceramics featuring religious symbolism first appeared around 800 CE, and the sculptures were developed by Spanish colonisers who replaced native gods with biblical figures, using the trees as teaching aids during missions. The Soteno family upended this colonial tradition, introducing garish colours and unorthodox characters that hark back to Mexico's Indigenous cultures. Jungle animals, fantastical beasts (not unlike Pedro Linares' alebrijes, p.120, by this point a staple of Mexican folk art), Aztec pottery, a string-playing mermaid (perhaps the Aztec water goddess Chalchiuhtlicue), maracas and more collide in a cornucopia of lush leaves and tropical flowers. It's a lively Garden of Eden, an explosion of texture and vibrancy that blends Gospel with pre-Christian Mexican worldviews.

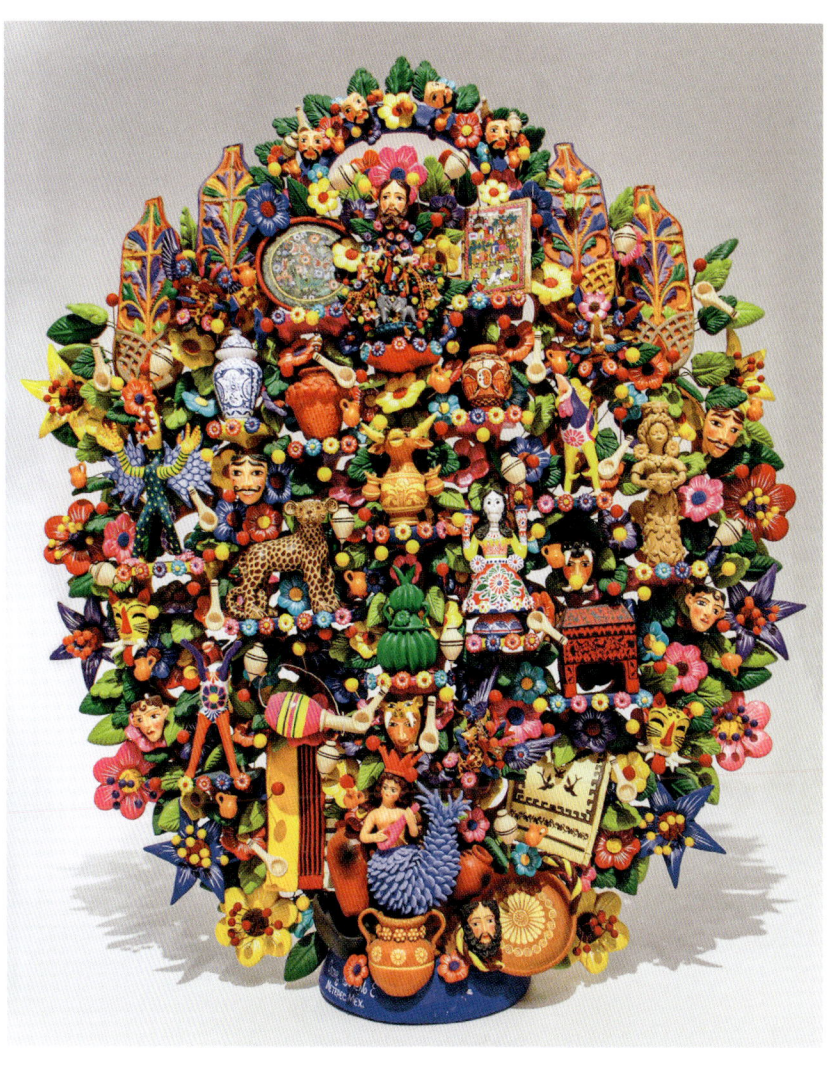

Oscar Soteno, *Tree of Life*, c. 2006, acrylic on ceramic, Museo de Arte Popular, Mexico City

FUSAKO AIZAWA

Temari Ball, 2000s

A ball of loyalty

By the time of Fusako Aizawa's first exhibition – on her 88th birthday – she had created nearly 500 handmade temari balls. Temari, meaning 'hand ball' in Japanese, are traditionally made from silk and intricately embroidered. The first temari were constructed from scraps of kimono formed into a sphere, and were supposedly wrapped so tightly that they could bounce. The balls became recognised as a nobility art form during the Edo period (1603–1868), with designs becoming ever more elaborate and requiring months of patient work to finish. They ceased to be used as toys during the 20th century, when rubber provided a springier, more durable alternative, but they remain an important example of Japanese folk craft. Incorporated in Japan's gift exchange culture, temari balls have been passed down from mother to daughter, from grandmother to granddaughter, often containing a secret wish written on paper and buried inside. This fractal ball depicts geometric flower patterns – one of many classic temari designs that Aizawa tried her hand at. Aizawa's granddaughter NanaAkua shared photographs of her grandmother's collection on social media and her posts went viral, sparking media coverage all over the world and demonstrating an enduring love for traditional art forms.

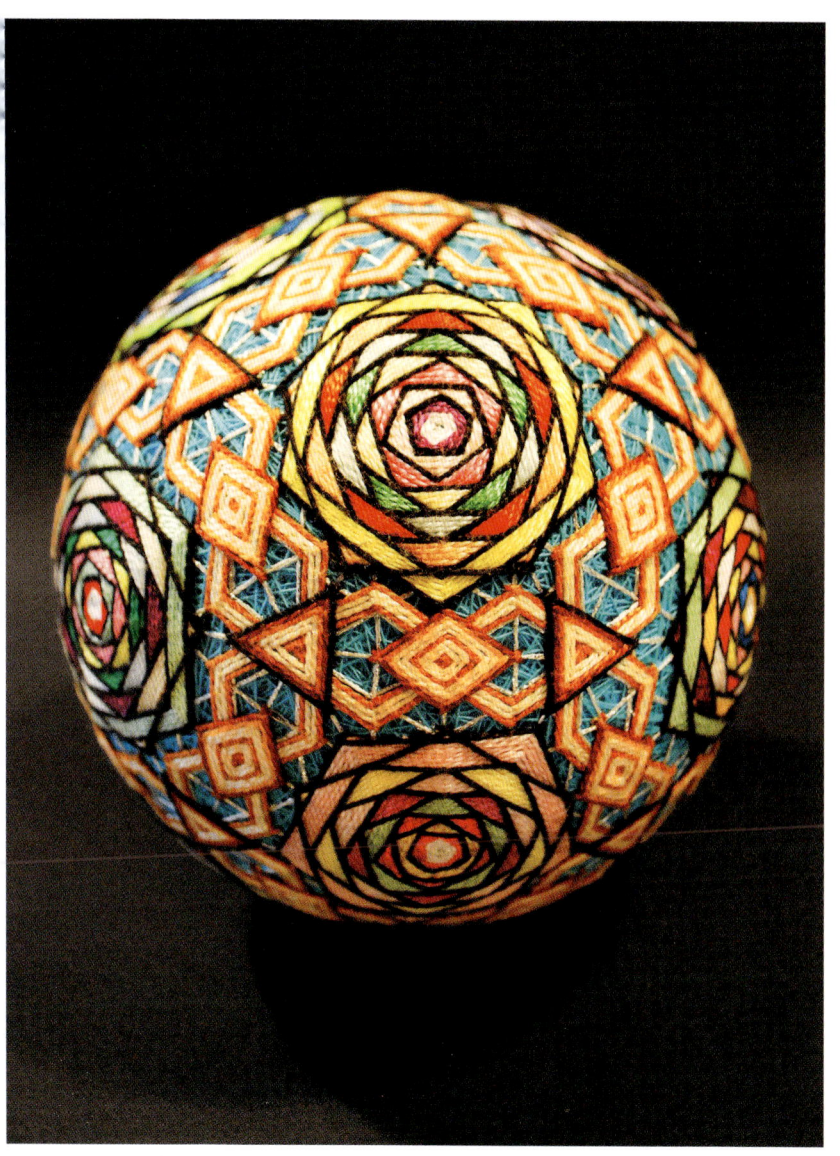

Fusako Aizawa, *Temari Ball*, 2000s

Marionette from *The Path to Cairo*, 2012

Ambitious retelling of history

Who is pulling the strings of history? This question haunts the work of Egyptian artist Wael Shawky, whose trilogy of horror films *Cabaret Crusades* explores the medieval religious wars from the vantage point of Arab historians. The Crusades (1096–1291) saw Christian armies unleashed to 'recapture' the Holy Land of Jerusalem from Muslim rule. Historically, the Crusaders have been a source of Western pride, with figures like Richard the Lionheart elevated to hero status. Among Arabs and Muslims, however, these events have long been steeped in shame and bewilderment. Set in an uncanny world inhabited by marionette puppets (made using 18th-century techniques), Shawky's films complicate the dominant historical narrative of the Crusades as a clash between East and West. All his characters speak Arabic, blurring the lines between the two sides. The decision to use string puppetry – a folk storytelling device found across many cultures – shows how folk objects and techniques can be absorbed by contemporary art to channel alternative narratives. Here, it is an exploration of control, a nod to the manipulation of reality by Western historians. The strings are clearly visible in the films, the actions of the characters directed by an unseen hand.

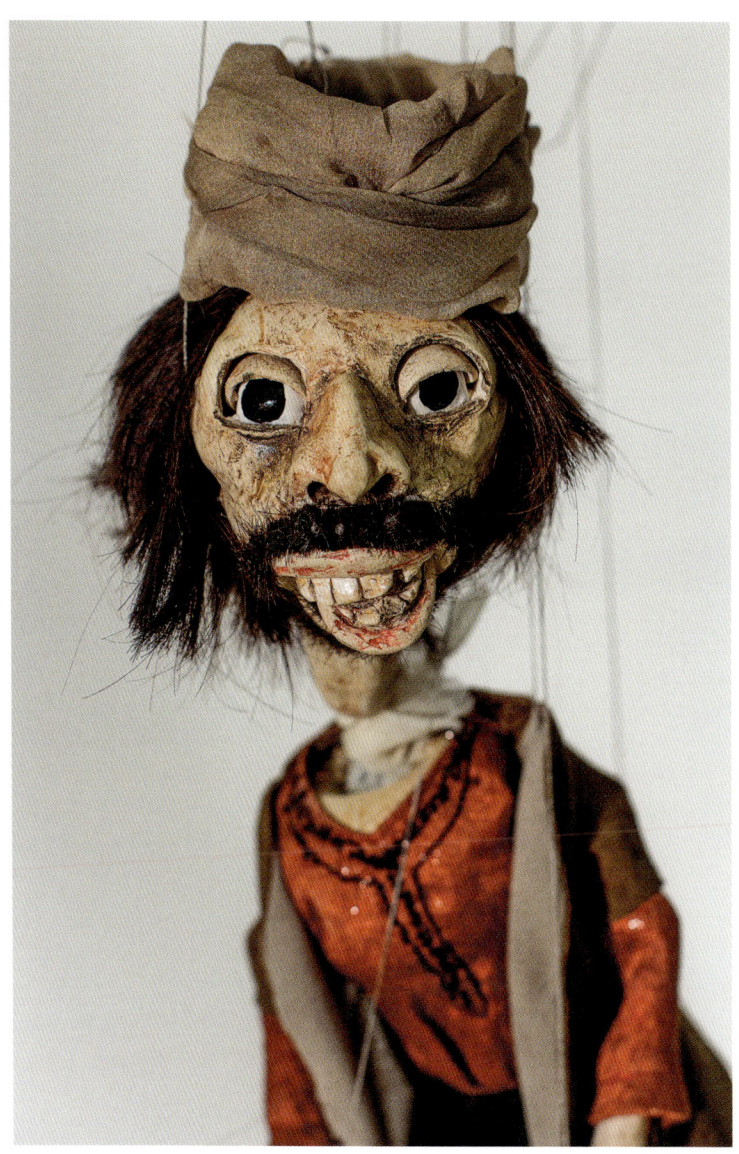

Wael Shawky, *Cabaret Crusades: The Path to Cairo*, Figure #3, 2012, 62 × 42 cm

DULARI DEVI

Prime Minister Modi Arriving in a Village via Helicopter, 2015

Landing a campaign trail

The controversial Prime Minister Modi and his entourage fly above crowds of reverent supporters in this painting. This is an example of Madhubani art – boldly coloured paintings traditionally created by women in the Mithila region of India and Nepal. But instead of depicting scenes from an ancient epic or a goddess descending upon her devotees, as is traditional in the genre, Dulari Devi chooses something more mischievous. Modi visited Devi's home state of Bihar in the lead-up to India's 2014 election. Gaining the state's support was crucial for his victory, and women – who turned up to vote in greater numbers than men – held the key. It is no accident that the supporters in this painting are all female, dressed in bright saris and with children milling about their feet. Devi is emphasising the increasing political participation of women, and especially low-caste Dalit women like herself, who put Modi in power based on his promises of economic prosperity for all. Despite the hope generated by Modi's campaign in this community, caste-based inequalities have remained deeply entrenched, the helicopter long departed.

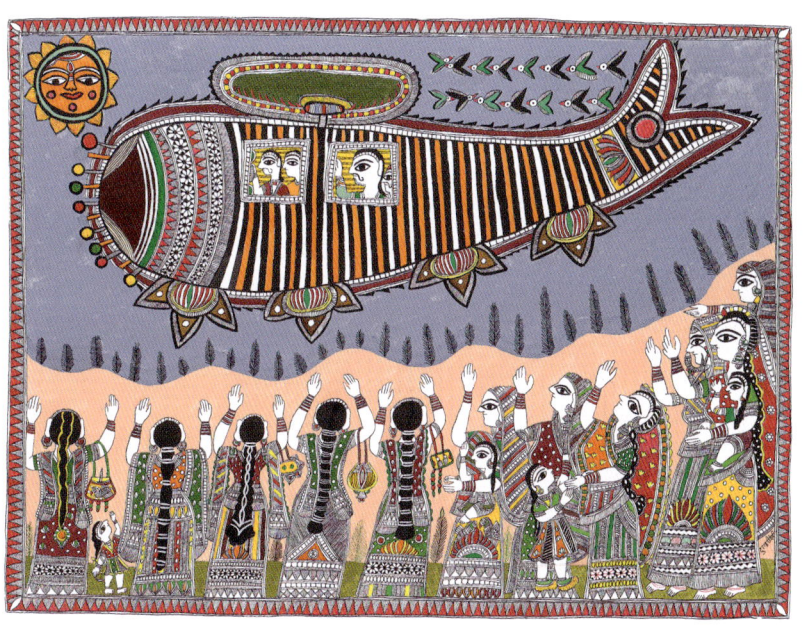

Dulari Devi, *Prime Minister Modi Arriving in a Village via Helicopter*, 2015,
ink and colours on paper, 55.6 × 74.9 cm, Asian Art Museum, San Francisco

KATRINA MAJKUT

In Control 5, 2017

My body, my voice

It represents a familiar object and a hard-won (and continually threatened) right for women around the world: a pack of 28 contraceptive pills. Ukrainian-American artist Katrina Majkut raised reproductive rights as a visual manifesto in *In Control*, an embroidery series started in 2012 to demystify objects related to women's menstruation, birth control, pregnancy and post-partum care. Central to folk art practices around the world, needlework remains an important medium of personal expression for women – from samplers stitched by 18th-century schoolgirls (p.52) to protest banners and handkerchiefs embroidered by suffragettes. Majkut's work is an affirmation of women's full sovereignty over their bodies, not only a record of the embroiderer's dexterity but also a poster for feminist art activism. This piece is particularly powerful: it coincided with Donald Trump's first presidency, which emboldened an anti-choice culture and saw reduced access to abortion in some conservative American states.

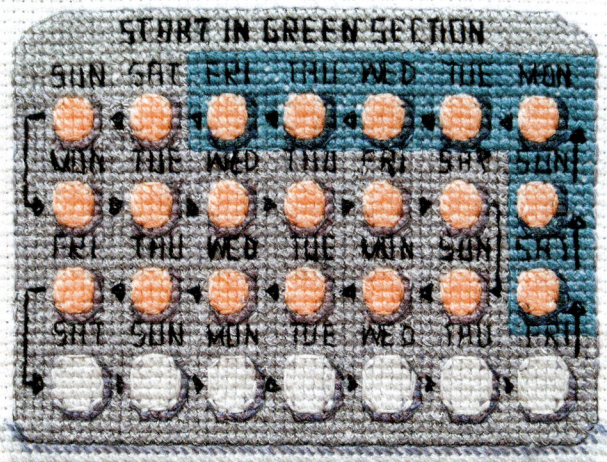

Katrina Majkut, *In Control 5*, 2017,
cross-stitched cotton embroidery thread on Aida cloth, 25 × 25 cm

NESPOON

Mostar Mural, 2021

Acknowledging the scars

Polish artist NeSpoon creates lace-inspired art around the world, covering buildings in lace (real and painted) to beautify public spaces. But there's a darker underpinning to this work. Painted onto the bullet-damaged wall of a building in Mostar, Bosnia and Herzegovina, the mural grapples with the visible scars left by the war of 1992–1995. 'It was one of the simplest [pieces of lace] I have ever painted. Emotionally – it was perhaps the most difficult project,' NeSpoon said. Mostar, a multiethnic city famed for its stunning Ottoman-era bridge, was besieged several times during the war, resulting in the displacement of most of the city's population, thousands of civilian casualties, the destruction of a huge number of buildings and untold psychological damage. Rape of Bosnian and Herzegovinian women was used by paramilitary forces as a weapon of war and key tactic in their programme of ethnic cleansing. NeSpoon chose to honour a local lace pattern as an homage to these women. 'I wanted not to think about it, but I did,' she said of the conflict. 'The bullet holes became part of my mural.' NeSpoon carefully painted around – rather than over – the building's visible damage, the lace design almost like applying a gauze dressing to a wound.

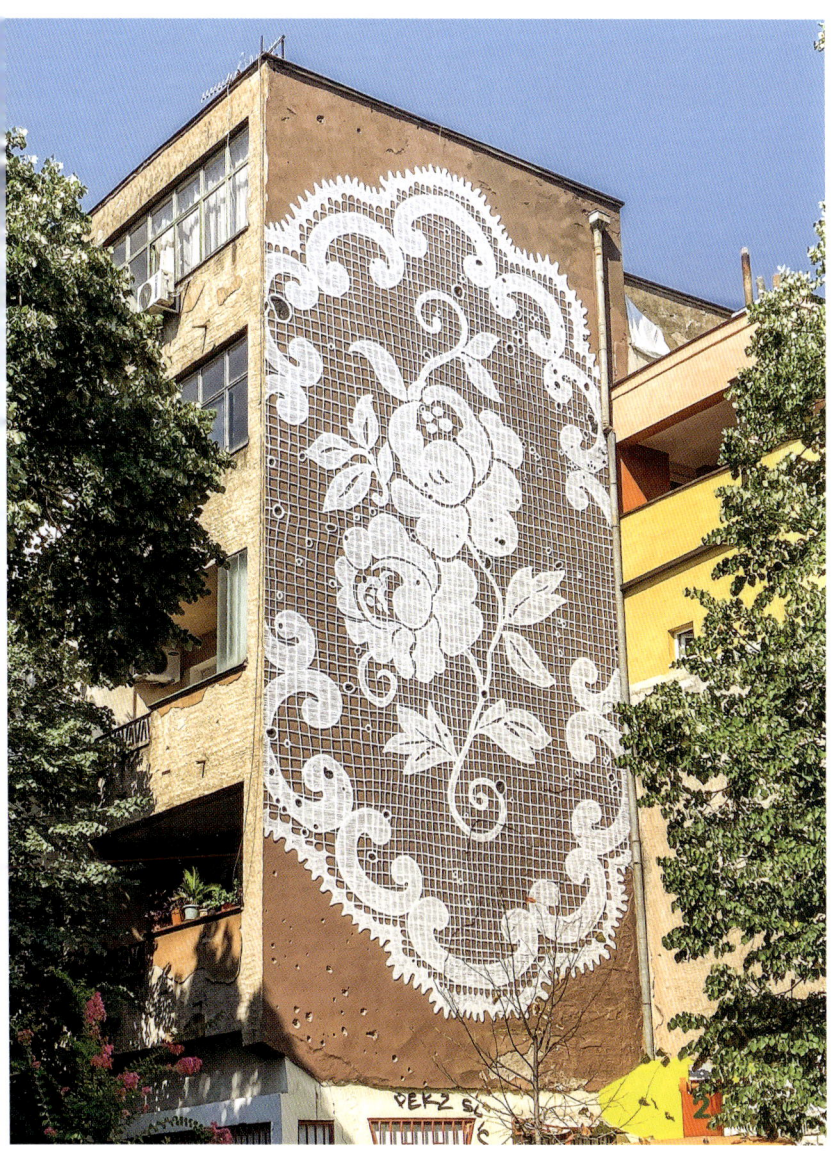

NeSpoon, *Mostar Mural*, 2021, Mostar, Bosnia and Herzegovina

Defiance, 2022

A symbol of resistance

Pysanky are eggs decorated using layers of wax and vivid dyes, a Ukrainian tradition that dates to pagan times. In these pre-Christian days, the eggs were created to honour the sun god and call for the rebirth of nature. Today, it's an activity associated with Easter, with eggs typically decorated with bright swirls, geometric shapes, flowers, pine branches, chicks, crosses and other symbols to signify harmony with the seasons. This one is less ornate. It features an abstract, faceless man missing a limb, the colours of the Ukrainian flag wrapping his remaining forearm. Artist Sofika Zielyk borrows iconography – the anonymous, armless silhouette – from Ukrainian-born avant-garde painter Kazimir Malevich, who was persecuted by Stalin for criticising the Soviet regime. Zielyk was inspired to paint this pysanka in September 2022, after the full-scale Russian invasion of Ukraine. Images circulated of a mass grave discovered in Izium, Ukraine, where hundreds of Ukrainian victims were shot with their hands tied behind their backs. Memorialising this tragedy by evoking Malevich's work of a century prior, Zielyk reminds us that artists have continually fought against brutal regimes. The pysanky are a symbol of this ongoing resistance and cultural preservation.

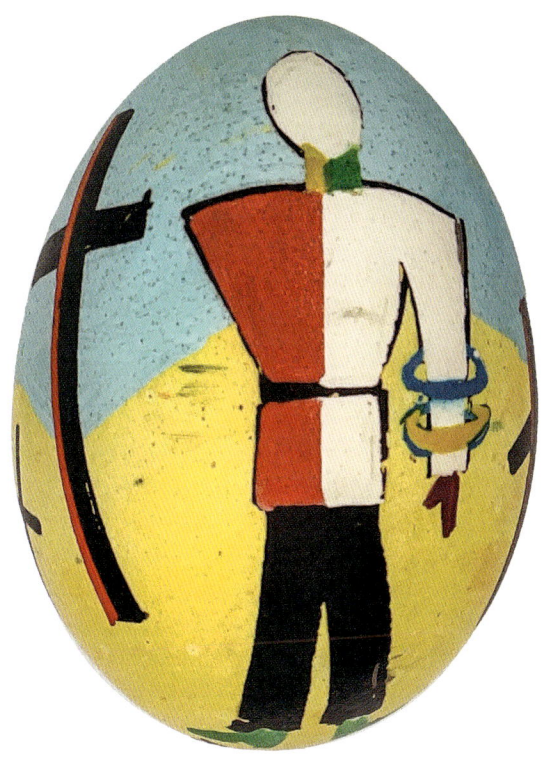

Sofika Zielyk, *Defiance*, 2022, chicken egg, batik

BEN EDGE

The Dorset Ooser, 2022

A celebration of English folk customs

Encountering this humanoid, horned creature means you're in trouble. The Dorset Ooser was a frightening timber mask found in the folklore of Melbury Osmond, a village in the English county of Dorset. The chilling effigy was used in ritualistic parades to shame community members deemed to have behaved badly (the village mob, banging pots and pans, can be seen to the left of the painting). Ben Edge has been interested in British folk culture since stumbling across a druidic ceremony in central London. A modern bard, his work resurrects a forgotten Britain, reminding us of over-looked enchanting stories and local heritage. Here, the Ooser towers over a quintessentially English landscape of rolling hills, backdropped by a glowing sunset. The centuries-old chalk figure of the Cerne Abbas Giant looms over a troupe of Morris dancers – another English folk custom that began in the 15th century and continues to this day. It's hard to tell what time period we are looking at, and that's the point: while the villagers' clothing looks medieval, closer inspection of the Ooser reveals he is wearing black lace-up trainers, inhabiting a strange, imagined world where old meets new.

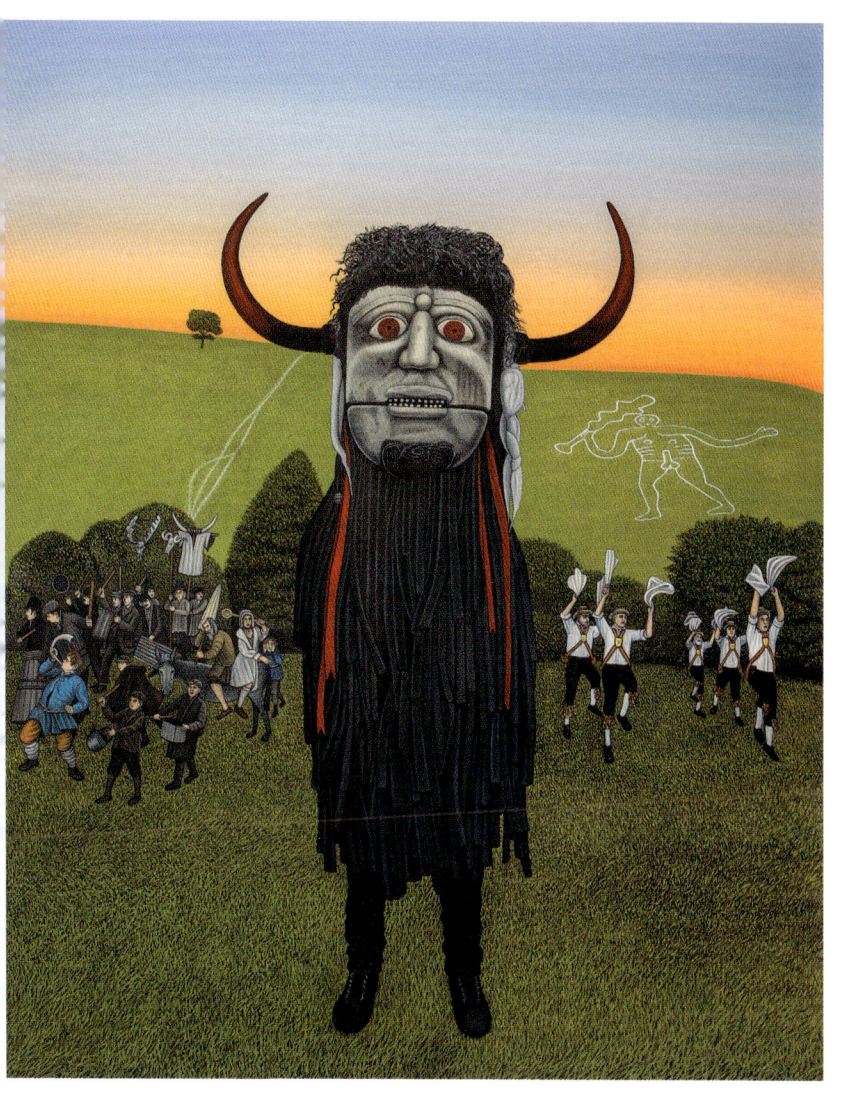

Ben Edge, *The Dorset Ooser*, 2022, oil on canvas, 100 × 80 cm

Truck, 2023

Paint my ride

Driving these large vehicles is not for the faint-hearted. Pakistani truck drivers are often absent from their homes for weeks or even months at a time, travelling long distances on unpaved mountain roads. And so, they turn to specialised workshops to personalise their vehicles with boisterous patterns and textures, incorporating decorative elements such as landscapes and idioms to remind them of what they've left behind. Influenced by the pre-existing practice of boat painting in Pakistan, truck art emerged soon after these trucks hit the road in the 1920s. Popular motifs include zesty floral patterns, calligraphy, religious or poetic verses, patriotic messages and animals, crafted and carved from wood, plastic and metal. Different regions have developed their own styles (woodwork is popular in Peshawar, while shiny stickers are a Karachi specialty). These striking ornaments not only serve as personal expression for the drivers, but ward off the evil eye with good-luck charms that keep them safe on the road.

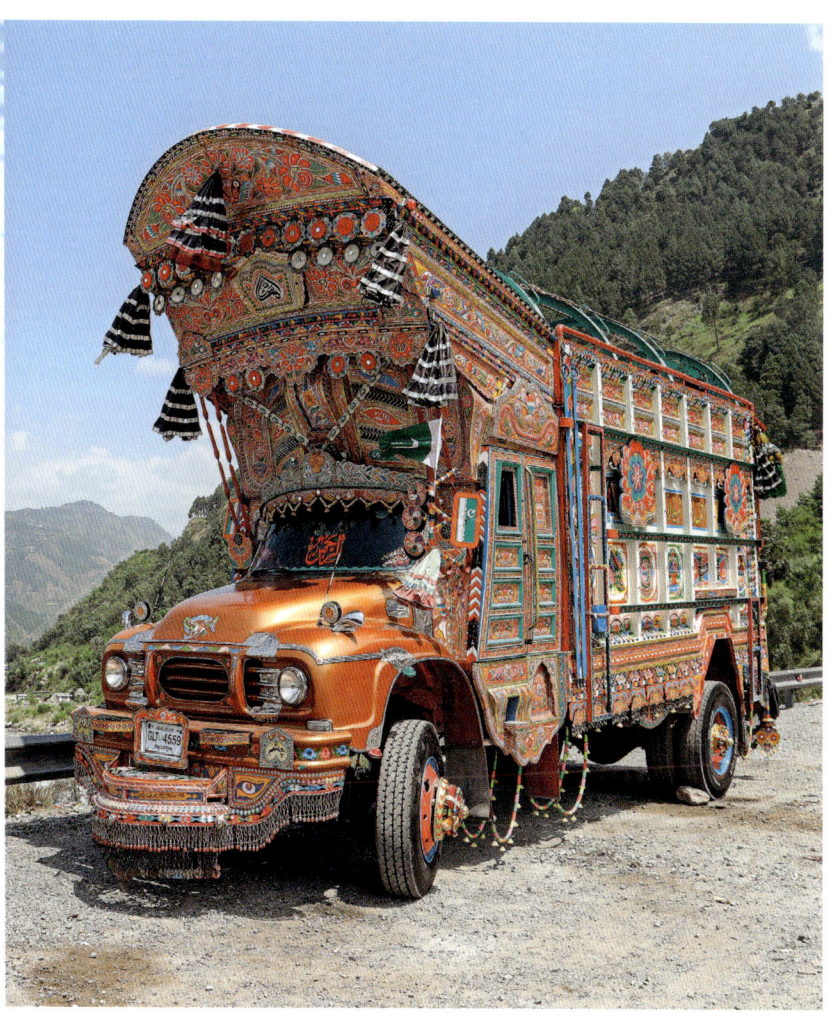

Truck, 2023, Pakistan

JORDAN NASSAR

A Mountain Looms, 2023

Palestinian tatreez as minimalist utopia

A mountain *looms* twice in this geometric artwork. Consider the grid as a whole and you'll see its looming silhouette, half obscured by patterned squares. And if you pay more attention to the individual grids, you might guess the labour of a weaver. The piece feels domestic – like ceramic bathroom tiles, or a patterned blanket, perhaps – but there is a political undercurrent. Jordan Nassar was born and raised in New York City, yet as a member of the vast Palestinian diaspora who collaborates with Palestine-based embroiderers, his work often straddles spaces. Here, he contrasts the domestic qualities of *tatreez* – an embroidery technique traditionally performed by Palestinian women in their homes – with the open landscape. This is a vast setting in which one can wander without obtaining permits or crossing endless checkpoints – otherwise frequent restrictions to movement for Palestinians. In Palestinian folk culture, tatreez has a dual function as both a clothing ornament and a language to convey information on ancestry, with motifs unique to specific villages, tribes and even families. Nassar subverts tradition by mixing patterns, creating an imagined, idyllic vision of Palestinian land.

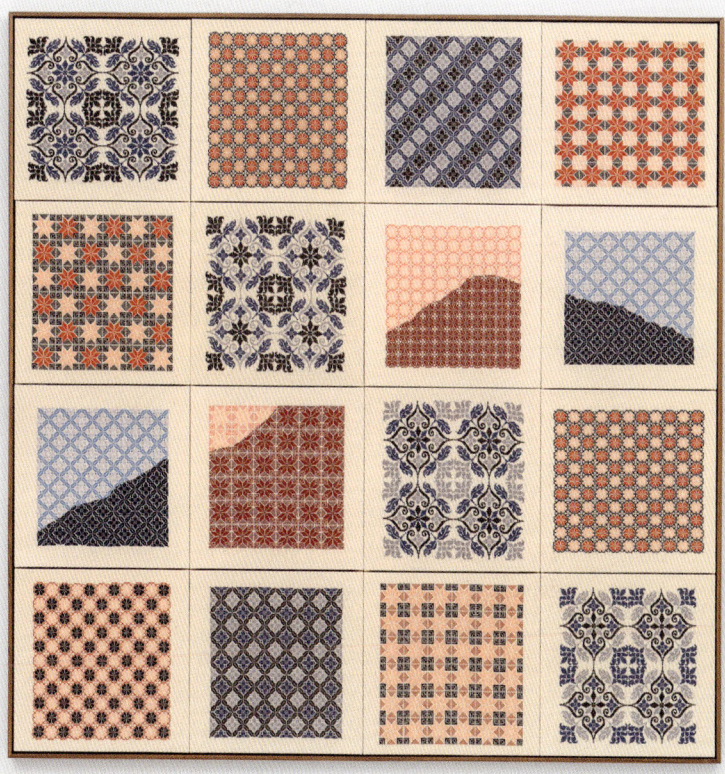

Jordan Nassar, *A Mountain Looms*, 2023, hand-embroidered cotton on cotton, 213.4 × 213.4 × 2.5 cm, private collection

Maman Monument Vivant, 2024

Child of the Republic

She stands out against the fancy Haussmann facades of Paris, far from her native Cameroon, with her baby wrapped tightly over her traditional pagne dress. In his work, Francis Essoua Kalu, a.k.a. Enfant Précoce ('precocious child' in French) explores his hybrid, diasporic identity as a French Cameroonian. Through cartoon-like vignettes, Enfant Précoce revisits his experience of otherness and family life, exposing France's persisting prejudices against people hailing from its former colonies. Fluid lines and bold colours recall the folk artistry and palette of his native Cameroon, and the painting bears the hallmarks of naivety shared by other self-taught artists. Here, Enfant Précoce's mother is visible, her appearance is exalted by the eyes of a loving son. The setting is cold and lonely, but in contrast with Paris's desaturated hues is her rich complexion, her fashionable green dress, heels, bling and make-up (manicured nails and all). She may be worn out by the relentless labour of existing in a new, intimidating country, resting on a plinth with her shopping caddy, but here she is a living monument to all immigrants, all the mothers working hard to make ends meet.

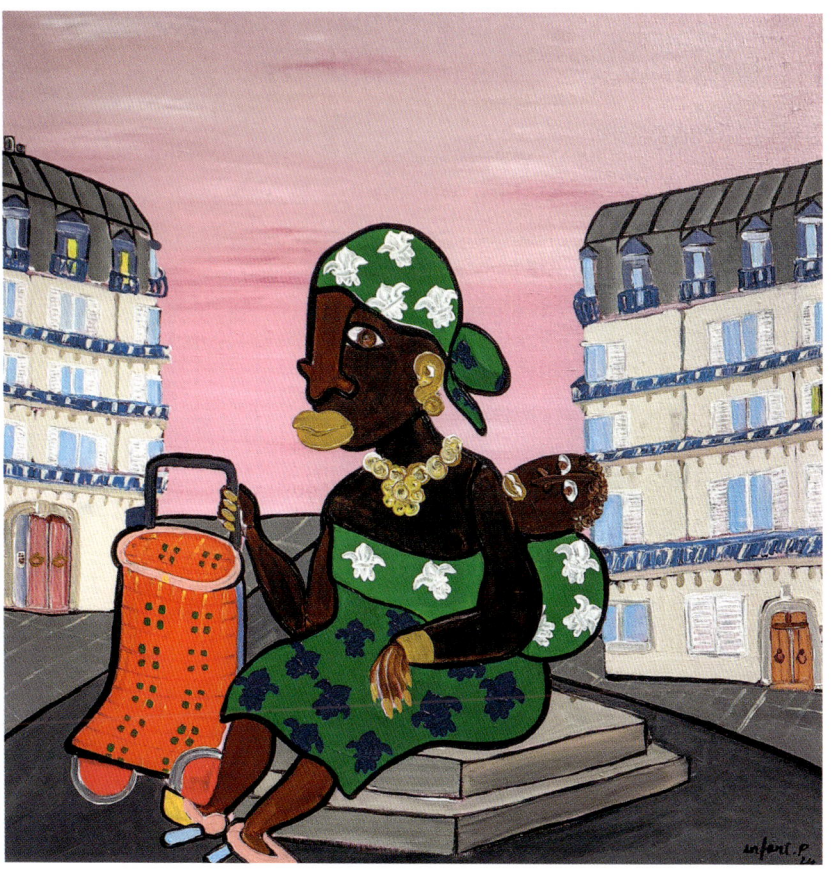

Enfant Précoce, *Maman Monument Vivant*, 2024, acrylic on canvas, 70 × 70 cm

Artist Directory

Fusako Aizawa
b.1922, Japan
d.2019, Japan
Beloved temari ball artist whose work went viral after her granddaughter documented her nearly 500-piece-strong collection of embroidered temari balls.

Baya
b.1931, Algeria
d. 1998, Algeria
A self-taught artist famed for her vibrant paintings blending African folklore, nature and feminine motifs, Fatima Haddad Mahieddine (known as Baya) is considered a key proponent of modern Algerian art.

Pieter Bruegel the Elder
b.c.1525–1530,
the Netherlands
d.1569, Belgium
A master of the Dutch Golden Age, Bruegel is renowned for his vivid landscapes and genre scenes depicting peasant life, full of humour and realism rendered with meticulous precision.

Dulari Devi
b.1968, India
A celebrated artist from the Dalit caste who pursues the communal tradition of Mithila paintings. Dulari's vibrant works offer a contemporary spin on the traditional art form, often from the vantage point of women.

Rosena Disery
b.1805, USA
d.1877, USA
A Black freeborn student at New York's African Free School, Disery completed an extraordinary sampler reflecting on abolitionist themes aged 15. She eventually married and had children, but unfortunately we lack recorded details about her life.

Ben Edge
b.1985, UK
Contemporary visual artist and musician, Ben Edge captures British folklore through his detailed paintings, combining mysticism, local traditions and social themes.

Enfant Précoce
b.1989, Cameroon
Francis Essoua Kalu, known as Enfant Précoce, is a contemporary artist who fuses street culture with personal narrative, exploring memory and identity in bold, vibrant renderings inviting us to engage with Black diasporic mythologies.

Safia Farhat
b.1924, Tunisia
d.2004, Tunisia
A socially conscious painter and designer, Farhat was a pioneering figure of Tunisian and Arab modern art, blending traditional North African motifs with modern aesthetics in tapestries and ceramics.

Ralph Fasanella
b.1914, USA
d.1997, USA
An American self-taught painter and union organiser, Fasanella depicted urban working-class life and labour movements. His attentive works reflect his political activism and unquenchable love for New York City and its people.

Denzil Goodpaster
b.1908, USA
d.1995, USA
A locally famous Appalachian folk artist who painted and carved wooden sculptures – including canes – depicting raw, quirky, expressive scenes from Americana lore.

Natalia Goncharova
b.1881, Russia
d.1962, France
Avant-garde visual artist and costume designer, Goncharova was a leading figure of modern art movements such as Futurism and Rayonism. Her work incorporates Russian folk traditions with modernist interpretations.

Otesia Harper
b.1925, USA
A Black quiltmaker from the American South tradition, Harper's quilts are known for their bold, graphic patterns, including high-contrast colours and punchy storytelling elements with cheeky overtones.

He Nupa Wanica / Joseph No Two Horns
b.1852, USA
d.1942, USA
Warrior–artist No Two Horns recorded the history of the Great Plains Indians – in war and resistance – through ledger art (narrative painting and illustrations on animal hides), creating poignant visual artefacts of survival and transformations in Lakota life.

Clementine Hunter
b.c.1887, USA
d.1988, USA
One of America's most iconic self-taught artists, Hunter chronicled plantation life in naive, vivid strokes. Using discarded materials, she preserved a vanishing world by painting from memory.

Joseph Jean-Gilles
b.1943, Haiti
Living most of his life in exile, Jean-Gilles channels Haitian primitive art in his lush, luminous scenes of rural life. A self-taught painter, he has exhibited in solo as well as group shows in the United States.

William H. Johnson
b.1901, USA
d.1970, USA
A major Black modernist painter, Johnson blended folk art and modernism. He experimented with expressionist paintings and sketches in his early career before turning to

the bold and colourful depictions of Black life and folk culture in America that made his work canonical.

Emily Kame Kngwarreye
b.1910, Australia
d.1996, Australia
An internationally celebrated Aboriginal elder and artist, whose monumental abstract paintings were inspired by sacred Anmatyerre culture representing mythical places. She co-founded Utopia Women's Batik Group in 1977 – an influential collective that propelled Aboriginal women in contemporary art.

Leonard Knight
b.1931, USA
d.2014, USA
Eccentric American folk artist, Knight created *Salvation Mountain* in the California desert: a massive installation expressing his religious faith through mounds of collected materials, achieving a boundless vision of community.

Pedro Linares
b.1906, Mexico
d.1992, Mexico
Linares is one of Mexico's most beloved folk artists, leaving behind an influential legacy with his alebrijes: fantastical beasts that appeared to him in a fever dream and which are now part of the country's national heritage and pride.

Katrina Majkut
b.1982, USA
A contemporary Ukrainian-American artist using embroidery as a medium for feminist activism. Majkut's works blur the line between domestic craft and political art, exploring reproductive health and social norms affecting women.

Jivya Soma Mashe
b.1934, India
d.2018, India
Mashe transformed the traditional tribal art form of Warli painting into a global phenomenon. This revival helped preserve a cherished Indian folk tradition.

Grandma Moses
b.1860, USA
d.1961, USA
An icon of 20th-century American folk art, Anna Mary Robertson Moses, known as Grandma Moses, began painting late in her seventies. Her pastoral scenes are full of nostalgia and simplicity, winning American hearts by capturing the essence of rural New England, American festivals, seasons and family moments.

William Murray
b.1756, USA
d.1828, USA
A painter and illustrator, Murray created sensitive

hand-painted family records in a style known as fraktur.

Jordan Nassar
b.1985, USA
A contemporary mixed-media artist from the Palestinian diaspora, Nassar's works are inspired by Palestinian culture and craft – including traditional embroidery – and engage with belonging and imagination.

NeSpoon
b. Poland
Polish contemporary street artist NeSpoon paints lace murals onto building facades to beautify public spaces, using traditional patterns to create site-specific installations.

Ammi Phillips
b.1788, USA
d.1865, USA
A prolific itinerant portraitist, Phillips painted hundreds of portraits with a distinctive realist style and soft, luminous tones using visual templates to easily recreate compositions.

Harriet Powers
b.1837, USA
d.1910, USA
Prominent Black quiltmaker from the American South, Powers championed the style of Bible quilts, depicting biblical and historical scenes with a unique, narrative touch inspired by African American oral storytelling.

Maria Prymachenko
b.1909, Ukraine
d.1997, Ukraine
Major Ukrainian folk artist Prymachenko created vibrant, fantastical paintings of animals and nature. Her work honoured local folklore, imagination and political themes with a bold gouache palette and intricate designs that pay homage to the country's vibrant cultural heritage.

Israel Dov Rosenbaum
Not a lot is known about 19th-century folk artist Rosenbaum, who created intricate designs blending Jewish mysticism and Eastern European Jewish ceremonial art. His papercut mizrah is kept in New York's Jewish Museum, and has influenced contemporary artists such as Kehinde Wiley.

Antonio Roseno de Lima
b.1926, Brazil
d.1998, Brazil
Brazilian folk painter of modest origins, Roseno de Lima celebrated the rhythms of life in vivid colours and expressive forms. His work is inspired by the vibrancy of Brazil's Nordeste region as well as a life mostly spent in poverty.

Henri Rousseau
b.1844, France
d.1910, France
A defining self-taught artist of the 20th century,

Rousseau's works of fantastical jungles and flattened perspectives influenced generations of modern artists. His work bridges naive art and modern avant-garde, creating a new, authentic visual language.

Wael Shawky
b.1971, Egypt
Mixed-media contemporary artist and filmmaker, Shawky's works investigate history, mythology and contemporary politics. His epic narratives challenge colonial legacies and cultural memory, blending fiction and truth. He represented Egypt in its national pavilion at the 2024 Venice Biennale.

George Smart
b.1774, UK
d.1846, UK
Smart was a tailor turned unlikely local folk artist. Using scraps of fabric, he created charming, textured collages of local characters and vistas, assembling endearing visions of English rural life.

Oscar Soteno
b.c.1970, Mexico
Belonging to a lineage of renowned ceramicists, Soteno creates intricate sculptures called 'trees of life' that incorporate Indigenous and biblical themes of creation myths and nature in rich, exuberant details.

Bill Traylor
b.1854, USA
d.1949, USA
Born into slavery, Traylor found his artistic voice late in life, chronicling Southern Black life in simple yet powerful forms. Now recognised as a major Black American folk artist, his works are imbued with memory and resilience.

Kitagawa Utamaro
b.c.1753, Japan
d.1806, Japan
A master of genre painting called ukiyo-e, Utamaro captured the spirit of Edo-period urban culture. His woodblock prints – including folklore, theatre actors, courtesans and demon spirits – are full of elegance and wit.

Charlie Willeto
b.1897, USA
d.1964, USA
A Navajo (Diné) medicine man and artist, Willeto carved wooden figures that straddle the sacred and the minimalist. He often used his works to barter for food.

Sofika Zielyk
b. USA
Zielyk is a Ukrainian-American artist who preserves the tradition of pysanky (intricately hand-decorated eggs) as a form of contemporary art, honouring their cultural symbolism of survival in the midst of war.

Picture credits

18–20: The Metropolitan Museum of Art; 22: The Cleveland Museum of Art; 24–36: The Metropolitan Museum of Art; 38: public domain; 40–46: The Metropolitan Museum of Art; 48: Image © The Metropolitan Museum of Art/Art Resource/Scala, Florence; 50: The Minneapolis Institute of Art; 52: Photography © The New York Historical; 54: public domain; 56: © Christie's Images / Bridgeman Images; 58: Detroit Institute of Arts; 60: The Jewish Museum, New York; 62: The Metropolitan Museum of Art; 64: Division of Home and Community Life, National Museum of American History, Smithsonian Institution; 66: © Compton Verney / Bridgeman Images; 68: The Metropolitan Museum of Art; 70: From the American Flag Collection of Kit Hinrichs. Photograph by Terry Heffernan; 72: © Galerie Gmurzynska, Cologne, Germany/Bridgeman Images; 74: © Bridgeman Images; 76: Image courtesy of Mingei International Museum; 78: Smithsonian; 80–82: Photo © Smithsonian American Art Museum/Art Resource/Scala, Florence; 84: Kallir Research Institute/© Grandma Moses Properties Co / Bridgeman Images; 86: Photograph courtesy of Museums.Co. © Estate of Ralph Fasanella; 90: Photo © Minneapolis Institute of Art / The Ethel Morrison Van Derlip Fund / Bridgeman Images; 92: Museum of International Folk Art; 94: © TobyPhotos / Alamy Stock Photo; 96: © incamerastock / Alamy Stock Photo; 98: Photo: Arnaud Conne, Digitization Workshop - City of Lausanne Collection de l'Art Brut, Lausanne; 100: Photo © Smithsonian American Art Museum/Art Resource/Scala, Florence; 102–104: Museum of International Folk Art; 106: Courtesy of Aïcha Filali, image courtesy of the Barjeel Foundation; 108: Courtesy of Mathaf: Arab Museum of Modern Art, Doha – Qatar; 110: © Maria Prymachenko, courtesy of the Prymachenko Foundation; 112: OAS AMA | Art Museum of the Americas Collection; 114: Museum of International Folk Art; 116: Courtesy of the National AIDS Memorial; 120: Museum of International Folk Art; 122: © LHB Photo / Alamy Stock Photo; 124–126: Photo © Smithsonian American Art Museum/ Art Resource/Scala, Florence; 128: Artwork © Emily Kame Kngwarreye/Copyright Agency. Licensed by DACS 2025. National Gallery of Victoria, Melbourne / Bridgeman Images; 130: Courtesy of the Museum of Art & Photography (MAP), Bangalore; 132: Photo © AlejandroLinaresGarcia; 134: Image courtesy of NanaAkua (nanaakua.jimdo. com); 136: Courtesy the artist and Sfeir-Semler Gallery Beirut/Hamburg; 138: Photograph © Asian Art Museum of San Francisco; 140: © Katrina Makjut; 142: © NeSpoon; 144: © Sofika Zielyk; 146: © Ben Edge; 148: © jackie ellis / Alamy Stock Photo; 150: Courtesy the artist and Private Collection, Photo by Dan Bradic; 152: Artwork © Enfant Précoce; Photo © ADAGP, Paris and DACS, London 2025.

An Opinionated Guide to Folk Art
First edition

Published in 2025 by Hoxton Mini Press, London
Copyright © Hoxton Mini Press 2025. All rights reserved.

Text by Farah Abdessamad
Editing by Florence Ward
Production design by Dom Grant
Series design by Tom Etherington
Proofreading by Gaynor Sermon

A CIP catalogue record for this book is available from the British Library.

ISBN: 978-1-914314-84-1

Printed and bound by PNB, Latvia

Manufacturer: Hoxton Mini Press, 104 Northside Studios,
16-29 Andrews Road, London, E8 4QF
www.hoxtonminipress.com

Represented by: Authorised Rep Compliance Ltd., Ground Floor,
71 Lower Baggot Street, Dublin, D02 P593, Ireland
www.arccompliance.com

Hoxton Mini Press is an environmentally conscious publisher, committed
to offsetting our carbon footprint. This book is 100 per cent carbon
compensated, with offset purchased from Stand For Trees.

Every time you order from our website, we plant a tree:
www.hoxtonminipress.com

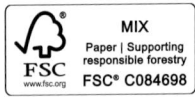

MIX
Paper | Supporting
responsible forestry
FSC
www.fsc.org
FSC® C084698